"Doc Reid's passion to see souls know Jesus is evident. He has dedicated decades of his walk with Christ toward the diligent work of evangelism. *Sharing Jesus without Freaking Out* is simply Doc's way of preaching what he practices. This text will enrich your walk, serve as a practical manual for those you teach, as well as mobilize saints from all walks of life to share the good news of the gospel we've been privileged to steward."

—**D. A. Horton**, pastor of Reach Fellowship and chief evangelist for Urban Youth Workers Institute

"Here is an extremely approachable and, at times, light-hearted approach to a deadly serious subject: telling others about your love for Christ without fear. I have given my life to the idea of one person lovingly and effectively telling another about the joy of walking with Jesus, and in this book, Alvin Reid does a superb job of helping you learn how to share your faith effectively. Fearlessly. I enthusiastically recommend it to you."

—**Rebecca Manley Pippert**, author of *Out of the Saltshaker and into the World*

"Let's face it: most Christians are freaked out when it comes to evangelism. We don't need someone scolding the ineffectiveness of the church today as much as a leader to show a fresh, effective way to tell the timeless good news. My friend Alvin Reid does just that in this encouraging book. You can have real and effective conversations with people about Jesus; Alvin will show you how."

—**Ed Stetzer**, Billy Graham Distinguished Chair for Church, Mission, and Evangelism and executive director of the Billy Graham Center for Evangelism at Wheaton College

SHARING
JESUS
{without *freaking* out}

ALVIN L. REID

SHARING JESUS

{without *freaking* out}

EVANGELISM
THE WAY YOU WERE BORN TO DO IT

B&H
ACADEMIC

NASHVILLE, TENNESSEE

Dedicated to my first grandchild, Lincoln.
May your generation show and share Christ
with conviction and compassion.

Contents

Preface

I've spent the past two and a half decades helping students, church leaders, and laypeople share their faith. During that time, I've learned a lot as well, although I have much to learn yet. Over twenty of those years I've taught at Southeastern Baptist Theological Seminary; more recently I also became a bi-vocational pastor, serving as pastor to young professionals at Richland Creek Community Church, a church planted in the late 1990s that has exploded in the years since. In the spring of 2015, I helped teach a class on Sunday nights focused on evangelism. As we talked about the name of the class, I didn't want to give it some boring title. Evangelism makes people nervous enough, so I sought a name that would encourage folks. I suggested calling it "Sharing Jesus without Freaking Out."

The result was the largest evangelism class on record at the church. Many attendees said they found the content to be encouraging, real, and helpful. This book is in part the product of that class, although it's even more a result of my years teaching seminarians.

In June of the same year, I found myself talking first with some colleagues and then with Chris Thompson of B&H Academic about the class. Both my colleagues and Chris encouraged me to write this book, and I'm grateful for the nudge. I make no claim to be the greatest soul-winner of my time, but I am a teacher, and a teacher is one who helps people get things. Many former students have also encouraged me to write an introductory book to help believers share Jesus confidently.

When I've told someone I was writing a book called *Sharing Jesus without Freaking Out*, it's elicited the same response each time: a chuckle followed by a statement like "That sounds like a book I need!" If you know Jesus, you know you should be sharing him with others, but the thought of doing so may freak you out on some level.

This book is not a comprehensive look at evangelism like my *Evangelism Handbook*. Rather, it has the specific focus of helping regular believers, from teenagers to senior adults, from homemakers to pastors, have real conversations with people about Jesus. I've written it as a conversation between the two of us, and I hope you will be encouraged, pushed just a bit, and grateful for this great message God has given us to tell to the world.

Acknowledgments

Our bodies represent a remarkable collection of inter-dependent systems, organs, and tissues; that's just the physical part. Intellectually, we have an unparalleled capacity compared to anything else in creation. Psychological, emotional, and relational features add to our complexity. Beyond this amazing and vast collection of all that makes each of us as a person, we are at our core spiritual beings created in the image of God for the glory of God to fulfill the mission of God.

Just as each person must be understood in terms of a multiplicity of factors, this book represents a myriad of influences on my life. People, strategies, and institutions have all contributed to my journey, and particularly to my training in evangelism. My debt for all I share in this work includes so many people it would take another, longer book to fill were I to thank each one. I've been blessed with remarkable teachers, pastors, mentors, friends, and models in sharing Jesus.

I want to thank Lane Harrison, a pastor and church planter, Mike Fry, our missions pastor at the Creek, and my accountability partner and fellow pastor and biker, Jim Gillespie for reading the manuscript and offering helpful and encouraging suggestions. My pastor, David Sims, and my president at Southeastern, Danny Akin, have been constant encouragers to me these years.

I also want to thank those who have been specifically helpful in the preparation of the book and pedagogical aids for its use. Micah Lang provided the excellent illustrations. Brian Upshaw and Matt Capps provided the means for me to videotape the training for the material you will read. Eric Stishan and Zach Petty helped with videotaping. Chris Thompson, Audrey Greeson, and Jennifer Day of B&H Academic have been helpful and encouraging throughout the process.

I'm particularly grateful to two groups: First, the multitude of students I've taught at Southeastern Seminary. Your response to your professor's teaching has been humbling. You have taught me more than I could ever teach you. Second, I thank God for the local church, particularly mine, Richland Creek Community Church. The pastors and staff love God, the sheep, and each other. Our Young Pros ministry, including both home group leaders and young professionals, has shaped me as a teacher and as a man. The concepts in this book were first taught in my classes and at my church, two wonderful laboratories for gospel-rich learning.

I'm most grateful for the gospel of Jesus, the glorious story we get to share, and my family—my wife, Michelle; our children, Josh and Hannah; their spouses, Jacqueline and Corey, and our first grandchild, Lincoln James Bolton. You are my rock and my joy.

Introduction

We met Marcy[1] on a Sunday in July when she showed up at our weekly young professionals gathering. This is hardly unusual, as new people join us all the time. But on her first day among us, Marcy broke into tears. That doesn't happen too often. Her sobs grew out of an unsatisfied life marked by pain—pain of a broken home and a broken life. But those tears also masked an even greater hunger: Marcy desperately wanted her life to matter.

She still believed the gap between the life she currently lived and the life she believed she was born to live could be crossed. She just didn't know how. That's when the reality of the good news of Jesus came alive to her. The gospel soothed her pain and gave her true hope. Her relationship with Jesus gave purpose to the passion in her soul. I baptized her later that summer in the lake (we do that annually at our church).

That was a few years ago. Today, Marcy is passionately pursuing her career, growing in Christ, and sharing him faithfully with others. Though she still has much to learn about Scripture and a Christian worldview, the pain Christ erased and the passion she now knows because of him have changed Marcy forever, and now she actively shares the good news with others.

Passion and Pain

Everyone you meet lives somewhere between the poles of passion and pain. They just got their dream job or a new house, were married, or had a baby. Or, conversely, they just lost their job, received some bad health news, or are experiencing deep hurt with a family member or friend. Sharing Jesus is as simple as connecting with others around their passion or their pain. It's in our everyday conversations that we can help people see that their life matters, that their passion to live comes from God, and that the good news of Jesus can rescue them from pain. That's what this book is all about—unpacking how to share our faith without freaking out.

In the following pages you will read about principles, eight in all, to help you share Jesus just the way God made you to be. Each principle is related to the others and is aimed at helping you see how God wired you to be you—how to be a living, loving witness without morphing into a person you were never meant to be. You don't have to be a superstar Christian or a clever communicator. You just need to find the intersection of your love for Jesus and your love for the other person. I want to show you how.

How to Read This Book

Every semester in evangelism class I ask my students to write down one of the following numbers: 1, 2, or 3. The numbers represent where they are as a witness.

1. Refers to a confident witness who has led people to Christ and trained others.
2. Signifies a believer who has shared the gospel more than a few times, but has yet to develop a consistent lifestyle of witness.
3. Represents a novice, someone who either has never been encouraged or trained to share Christ or is generally too afraid to try.

Where would you put yourself on this scale? Maybe a 1.5 or a 2.5? (That's okay.) If you are a 1, much of this will not be new, but there may be ideas that can help you or push you further in a specific area of your witness. This book can help you mentor or equip another believer or a group.

If you are somewhere around a 2, this book will give you a way of thinking about sharing Jesus that you will hopefully find refreshing and quite doable. You will be reminded why we share Christ and given practical ways to develop a lifestyle of witness that fits who God made you to be.

If you are a 3, perhaps a new or young believer, don't freak out! Take in all you will read. See the beauty of Jesus and his story in its reality. Pay particular attention to chapter 2, and to the eight principles shared throughout the book. Put into practice the application, found at the end of the book, and see what you can learn.

Regardless of where you fall on the evangelism spectrum, you can approach this book in a couple of ways. You can read it in a day or two or in bite-sized chunks over a longer period of time. I encourage you to walk through it slowly, a chapter a week, preferably with another person or with a group. At the end of the book you'll find an eight week challenge, which will provide you with an opportunity to grow in your witness. This is no "sink or swim" approach to growing as a witness. It aims to help you develop a lifestyle of sharing Jesus over time. Also, as you read, follow the link to bhacademic.com/sharingjesus for additional videos and resources. My hope is that the words you read and hear will help you learn how to share your faith more intentionally. And my prayer for you echoes Paul's prayer in Philemon 1:6: "that your participation in the faith may become effective through knowing every good thing that is in us for the glory of Christ."

{ CHAPTER 1 }

Spread the Word:
Don't Overcomplicate It

While Paul was waiting for them in Athens, he was deeply distressed
[that is, he was FREAKED OUT] when he saw that the city was
full of idols.

—Acts 17:16

What freaks you out?

We all freak out over one thing or another, sometimes for understandable reasons—if you are alone when a
zombie apocalypse breaks out, by all means, freak out—or
sometimes for really silly ones.

The media seems designed to freak us out. We have twenty-
four-hour news channels that by their very nature focus on the
latest tragedy or extreme news story, replaying it over and over.
We also see things on social media from the hilarious to the
frightening, pushing us closer to the freak-out zone.

A snake will do it for more than a few. That's true for my
wife, Michelle.

About a year ago I sat in our living room watching a ball game. Michelle has created a micro deer farm of sorts in our side yard. Deer abound in our neighborhood; Michelle feeds them, talks to them, and names them. She is Snow White: the deer hear her voice, and she calls them by name.

On a pretty typical July night, she sat on the tailgate of our old truck watching the deer as I enjoyed my game. Suddenly my cell phone rang; I looked to see the name flashing on the screen.

It was Michelle. Just outside.

We'd been married more than thirty-five years, which means you start to figure things out. Like that my wife never calls my cell phone when she is sitting just outside. As teens our kids texted their friends while sitting in the same room, but we prefer talking to each other.

Almost immediately I surmised why she used the cell rather than walking in to get me: it had to be a snake.

I hit the green button.

"Snake!" was about all I heard, so out the door I ran.

Sure enough, it was a snake, but not your garden-variety, friendly, neighborhood black snake.

The snake I spotted was most malevolent: a copperhead. The rusty serpent slithered across our driveway, where Michelle saw it below her feet as they dangled off the tailgate—that is, until she saw the snake!

Does that picture freak you out?

Snakes don't freak me out. I actually like snakes. I've kept a variety as pets. When I saw the pernicious pit viper, my first thought was to pin its head down, pick it up, and show its fangs on a video, proudly posting my biblical directive to take dominion on social media.

I did mention I have been married over thirty-five years, right? Since I would like to be married another thirty, I forgot the video idea, grabbed a golf club, and smote the serpent. I went Genesis 3:15 on him and crushed his gnarly head. I killed the dragon and rescued the girl. You get the idea.

Most people don't like to be freaked out like that. Sure, some of us occasionally like to be freaked out, like teens watching a horror movie.

I'm not sure what freaks you out. But if you're a follower of Jesus and really want to be freaked out, picture walking up to someone to boldly tell him about Jesus. You know, like talking to your church-loathing coworker, atheist family member, or that neighbor (the one who freaks you out).

I've preached or taught in more than two thousand churches, and trained in countless events involving everyone from middle school youth to church leaders. I've spent a lot of time interacting with and talking to Christians, from those who witness consistently to those who share Jesus about as much as they skydive. I'm convinced of this: most believers today really do love Jesus, really want to walk with him, and yearn to honor him.

You want to serve Jesus faithfully and live for him effectively, but you may not always know how.

Is it by making bold statements about political issues on social media?

Is it by posting online your outrage over the moral decline happening all around us?

Is it by separating your life and your family as much as possible from everything and everyone who does not love our Jesus?

Is it by being a good, church-attending, Bible-embracing, morally upright citizen, and nothing more?

What if I told you the God who spoke and created the universe made you uniquely in his image, in such a way that you—uniquely from everything else in creation—can worship, glorify, and serve him, and that we've overcomplicated things?

What if I showed you from God's Word that you and I were in fact made by God not only to be redeemed by Christ to glorify him and to serve him in the church, but what if I told you he made you—from the circumstances of your life to the people you know—to be a beacon of good news, and this too is both for his glory and for your good?

What if you saw how the passion of your life—those things that bring you joy, that turn your crank, that bring you great satisfaction—were given to you by God to be used for something bigger, to spread his fame?

Journey to Joy in Witnessing

I want to take you on a journey to see things afresh. God is on the move in our time, and we owe it to him, to others we influence, and to ourselves to be a part of his mission in the world.

How have we created a version of Christianity that makes us freak out over telling the best news in the history of the universe? Why would we get so tongue-tied and introverted when talking about the very thing Jesus came to do for us? How can we sing so joyfully about the gospel in a worship service and then be just as tight-lipped about Jesus in our workplace?

How can we be so quick to speak about a million other things that mean pretty much nothing special but cannot seem to talk about the message that set us free? How can we learn to share Jesus by both word and deed without freaking out?

I have good news. No, this is not a gospelized version of those bogus diet schemes guaranteed to get you to lose weight and feel great with no cost. Following Jesus costs you everything. It's not a three-step quick fix to easy Christianity, and it's not bait-and-switch. It's also not a program to suddenly turn you into the next Marvel superhero version of soul-winning amazement.

Part of the reason believers struggle with this comes from the very way we church leader types have taught people like you to share Christ. Let me say how grateful I am for so many who have taught me so much about telling the good news. At the same time, I've observed some unintended consequences of the way we have often packaged our evangelism training. We must constantly assess the effectiveness of what we do in growing disciples. Despite all the remarkable programs we have in evangelism, a LifeWay study showed 61 percent of evangelical Christians had not told a soul about Christ in the previous six months.[2] The good news is that the younger Millennial generation shows a higher rate of witnessing than older believers. Millennials demonstrate a burden for social justice as well, but according to a recent Barna report, not at the expense of evangelism.[3] More troubling in the LifeWay study is the discovery that out of eight attributes of growing believers, sharing Jesus ranked at the bottom. Why is evangelism ranked so low? Here are a few thoughts as to why, and it relates to how we teach believers to witness:

First, most believers do not consider themselves public speakers. According to Gallup, public speaking is the second-greatest fear of adults (second to the fear of snakes, by the way, although a more recent survey had public speaking virtually tied with a fear of heights as second).[4] Giving a set gospel presentation represents a form of public speaking more than an everyday conversation. This is a reason we've had so many people learn a plan to share Christ but never actually develop a lifestyle of witnessing.

Second, most of the folks who teach evangelism training tend to be aggressive, type A folks (raising my hand, guilty as charged) who share Christ passionately and genuinely want others to as well. But most people aren't wired like that, so it can be intimidating. Imagine you finally decided to get in shape. You go to a gym and hire a personal trainer, and out walks a guy who looks like Arnold Schwarzenegger's muscle-bound big brother. I would feel pretty defeated looking at myself in the mirror and then looking at that, wouldn't you?

Third, I've met too many Christians who tell me some version of this: "I met the Lord and started telling others how he changed my life. Then I took evangelism training and suddenly began to wonder if I was doing it all wrong. So I became more apprehensive than bold." That's not what is intended in witness training, and it's not what we are going for here. That may not be your story, but it's one I've heard far too many times.

A fourth reason I meet a lot of believers who struggle with witnessing has nothing to do with any kind of training, but with the Christian subculture we have created today, which leads the vast majority of Christians to spend most of our time around saved people, with little interaction with lost people. We live in Christian bubbles, which means we go to movies with believers, have parties with believers, and do pretty much everything in our discretionary time with believers. In our mastery of fellowship with the saints, we've lost a burden for a friendship with sinners. But Jesus was known as a friend of sinners (Luke 7).

> In our mastery of fellowship with the saints, we've lost a burden for a friendship with sinners. But Jesus was known as a friend of sinners (Luke 7).

I'm not going to try to make you the next Billy Graham or apostle Paul, but to help you become the person God made you to be, to become the person God created you to be, and to be like the host of believers in Scripture and history who tell the real story behind the spread of the gospel of Jesus around the world. Folks like those unnamed guys in Acts 11:19–23 who planted the gospel deeply in Antioch, the fourth-largest city of the Roman Empire. People like those Michael Green described in his book *Evangelism in the Early Church:* "In contrast to the present day, when Christianity is highly intellectualized and dispensed by professional clergy to a constituency increasingly confined to the middle class, in the early days the faith was spontaneously spread by informal evangelists, and had its greatest appeal among the working classes."[5]

These "informal evangelists" were normal people just like you (I'm talking about you) whom God used to evangelize the

Roman Empire. A reason we've not done so well at reaching America in recent years is we've lost personal ownership of the mission. We can do events that bring in crowds while blowing up our budgets. But in so doing we continue to keep most Christ-followers from the very thing God created us for: to proclaim his glory.

Evangelism Reboot

In every chapter I'm going to give you a statement to focus on, to encourage and to challenge you, starting with this one.

Principle 1: God created you for his glory, to advance his gospel with the gifts, talents, and opportunities he gave to you.

The same God who made the world and sustains all things made you in his image, or the *imago Dei*. His purpose for you and for me is both for his glory and for our good. We need to reboot our understanding of evangelism.

Sharing Jesus should not look like this: Say you are a guy who's been timid when it comes to witnessing. You've decided you are going to share Jesus with your neighbor. You know, that neighbor. His name is Bart. You've gotten to know him a bit but not as well as you should. You've only been in his house once, that time you came to welcome his family to the neighborhood.

But now it's time. Time to do the Jesus thing. Until now you assumed he is a normal dude, a guy who works hard and is generally a decent human being. But now you are meeting him for coffee to get to know him better as a friend, and to share with him the hope you have in Jesus.

Your mind begins to wander. *What really goes on in his house? His garage? He keeps it closed a lot, after all. There's something not right there.*

You start to have images of Walter White in *Breaking Bad*. *No, he is not normal after all. Suspicious, in fact. He probably has a meth lab in that garage. That's it, a meth lab. This man is dangerous. Dangerous! And you are meeting him for coffee! He will likely get mad;*

he may even go mental in the coffee shop. He may do worse. He knows where you live, remember?

The more you think about it, embarrassment is the least of your fears.

You have gone from a normal sense of nervous conviction to speak to your neighbor about Jesus to hallucinating about your now-terrorist neighbor's endangerment of your family. That's not going to help you help him see Jesus.

Or let's say you are a lady with a friend at work who is obviously not a follower of Jesus. You are burdened for her, so you invite her to lunch, and she agrees.

Then you begin to think. Or overthink, actually. *I want to talk to her about Jesus, but I didn't tell her that when I asked her to lunch. Maybe I should have?*

The closer to lunchtime, the more your fears grow. You realize you've only been at the job for a few months; she's worked there for years. Everybody knows her. She has lots of influence. *What will she say about you when you (gasp!) talk about Jesus? It could cost you your job!*

Okay. Stop it. Stop turning your next conversation into another episode of *CSI: (Your City)*. I've been sharing Christ for a long time, and I've made a multitude of friends and very few enemies as a result. Most folks I talk to are actually interested in spiritual things.

Let's replay these scenes.

You meet Bart for coffee. You have a nice conversation, and learn about things you had no idea you had in common (except that he loves the Patriots and you are a Steelers fan, but that's hardly the same as him running a meth lab). You tell him about your family, things that matter. You mention how important your faith is, and you talk to him about Jesus, including your own testimony of salvation. He doesn't respond with a desire to follow Jesus; he also doesn't take out a contract with a hit man on you for daring to speak of Christ. He respects your beliefs, says he's not there yet, but he is open to talking more.

You have crossed a barrier in sharing Jesus. And you have made a better friend. I would call that a win-win. Your confidence is growing!

And for the lady: You meet for lunch. You ask her about her story; turns out she seems comfortable enough with you to crack the door to share some pain in her life. You become transparent, telling her of some misfortune you too have had to face. Your vulnerability opens her up more to you.

"How did you make it?" she asks.

"I didn't," you reply. "At least, not alone." You tell her you believe there is more to this life than meeting obstacles and pursuing a career, that God made a remarkable world and made us uniquely to know him, but sin screwed up everything, including each of your lives.

She is, to your hidden surprise, listening closely. You keep talking, telling her you still struggle and you are far from perfect, but Jesus' death and resurrection changed everything for you. You are no theologian, you assure her, but you know Jesus has changed your life, your perspective, and your hope.

You look at her, surprised to see she is misty-eyed.

She opens up to her desire to know God, and you have the joy of leading her to Jesus.

Right there, on the spot.

"No, that won't happen," you say.

I would say it's more likely than the first scenario I painted.

Lost people are more amazed at our silence than offended at our message.

I want to help you to have real conversations with real people about a real Savior they genuinely need. It's also going to help you have normal conversations with normal people about our remark-

> Lost people are more amazed at our silence than offended at our message.

able Lord to give them a new-normal way to live. I want you to see Jesus and your relationship to him in a new, fresh light, moving you to a place where one day, instead of thinking of sharing Jesus as something somewhere between awkward and terrifying, it would be weird *not* to talk openly and consistently about Jesus.

The Right Kind of Freaking Out

Maybe we actually need to freak out a little bit, but only about things that matter. In October 2014, I visited San Francisco for the first time. I typed these very words in a coffee shop there. The first place I had to go was the corner of Haight and Ashbury streets. This street corner represents the epicenter of the hippie culture of the 1960s, and there was a hippie playing a guitar when I arrived, right on cue.

This is also where the earliest signs of what would be called the Jesus Movement began. A hippie named Ted Wise got saved, and then others joined him. Before long the movement went south, where a man named Chuck Smith and a church called Calvary Chapel exploded. Thousands of youth came to Christ, while at the same time thousands of youth in established churches experienced a new zeal for Jesus. Churches filled with youth groups, and Bill Bright of Campus Crusade for Christ (now Cru) organized an event called Explo '72 where eighty thousand young people came to Dallas, Texas, to learn to share Christ. On the Saturday following the event, some 150,000–180,000 youth gathered for a massive festival featuring Billy Graham, among others.

I was saved in those days. I remember young people who did not have a church background, who didn't have a lot of theological training—okay, they had none—but who had a passion to tell others about Jesus. We had a name for them: Jesus Freaks.

A Jesus Freak is someone who loves Jesus more than you do.

It's time to recapture the spirit of the Jesus Movement, to rekindle a passion for Jesus that spills out of hearts of love for God and others, and brings joy to those around us.

I want to help you share Jesus without freaking out. But what I really hope will happen is that God will so stir your soul that you can't help but talk about Jesus. We should be freaked out about the fact that men and women, boys and girls are headed to hell. We should be freaked out from a sense of urgency to tell the good news to our neighbors and to all nations. I hope we see a new generation of Jesus Freaks who freak out about things that matter. Like those earliest Jesus Freaks, Peter and John, who said in Acts 4:20, "We are unable to stop speaking about what we have seen and heard," my prayer is as you read and put to practice what you read, God will ignite a passion and give you direction in a way that you are never the same.

An Evangelism Catechism

Before we launch out on this journey together, let me walk you through a brief evangelism catechism. A catechism refers to a series of questions and answers as a teaching tool.[6]

Why do you and I exist?

God created us to know him and bring him glory. We long to say with Paul that we desire Christ to be "highly honored" by us (Phil 1:20). One of the ways we bring him glory is to make his salvation known to the ends of the earth (see the Great Commission in Matt 28:19–20). Neither you nor I are responsible for whether or not we lead anyone to Christ. God saves people. Salvation is way above our pay grade; it cost the Son of God his very life. But we do bring him glory—great, glorious glory—when we share his love and grace with others.

Witnessing starts with understanding what God does and what we do. God the Father saves; God the Holy Spirit convicts of sin (John 16:8–11); God the Son died and rose for our salvation. We open our mouths and talk about this, and we live our lives to reflect this. We are Plan A to reach the world, and God hasn't given us a Plan B.

Why do we do good works, including telling others about Jesus?

Our good works bring glory to God. We don't do good works to earn anything from God. We can't earn anything from God! But we do good works because God is good and we want to be like him. We also do good works to show others the reality of Christianity in our lives. Jesus said in Matthew 5:16: "In the same way, let your light shine before others, so that they may see your good works and give glory to your Father in heaven."

> God does not need our good works, but our neighbor does.

As Martin Luther observed, God does not need our good works, but our neighbor does.[7] It's our role to show and share the good news, something God created us to do. I've met so many people who feel like they fail in their witness because they base their success on the response of the other person, or base their walk with God on the results of their witness. If you know Jesus, you are all his. Guilt is forgiven, and sin is cleansed. Through Christ you are accepted. Do the good works you do, like living a life of character, showing compassion to the broken, and speaking openly of Jesus, out of a heart of gratitude and affection to God.

What is our primary role in sharing Jesus?

We proclaim the good news of Jesus' death and resurrection as clearly as possible through both our lips and our lives. That means it's not your job or mine to answer every question unbelievers have. Release yourself from the pressure of being the Bible Answer Man. The Bible's purpose is not to be a reference book or an answer to a list of spiritual FAQs. The Bible is God's revelation to us, revealing to us who he is, his great character, and his great plan of redemption. The Scriptures are not primarily about *morality*, but about *reality*. You and I are commissioned by the very Jesus who made all creation to proclaim his salvation, not to answer every question. We do want to help people with genuine questions as we can. I'll talk about that a bit later. We have a Great Commission (Matt 28:19–20) from our King, and the commission is to make disciples as living witnesses to the world (Acts 1:8). We do this from the perspective of the Great Commandment: to love God and love people (Matt 22:37–40).

Embracing Evangelism

For many of us, witnessing is uncomfortable. It's a "have to," not a "get to." But instead of seeing your witness as one more box to check on the road to Christian growth, I hope you learn to love fishing as much as catching. In Matthew 4:19, Jesus said, "Follow me, and I will make you fish for people!" In other words, followers are fishers!

Michelle and I love to fish. Okay, she loves to fish; I only love to catch fish. When we fish at the lake, I will fish a long time if they are biting. But if not, after an hour or so, I leave the pier, go hang up a hammock, and read a book. Michelle can fish all day and catch nothing. She fished regularly for a year before she caught what she sought: a bass big enough to mount on the wall. Michelle loves fishing as much as (or more than) catching. Applying this to our witness, if we can get to the place where we just enjoy being used by God to nudge people toward him, we will "catch" people for him!

Most of us fear being a failure at witnessing and rejection by others. I struggle with these too. Our confidence is not in ourselves, but in the gospel and in who God made us to be. The only "failure" in witnessing is the failure to witness, and even when that happens God still loves you. I've missed more opportunities than I've taken over the course of my life, but God still uses folks just like you and me. I want to encourage you to begin praying a simple, daily prayer. It's one I've encouraged my students to use for years. Here it is: "God, give me today

(1) an opportunity to speak with someone about Jesus; (2) the wisdom to see it; and (3) the courage to take it." Talking with God regularly about our witness helps overcome our fears of witnessing to others.

What if I told you the very fears you have can actually help you to grow? We actually love ambiguity and uncertainty more than we realize. If every painting were simply a single color, no one would like it. Imagine going to an art gallery and viewing a host of paintings, all of which were a white canvas. Would that be intriguing? No, it's the contrast of colors that makes a painting remarkable. Or, what if a song had one note? (Have you ever sung next to a loud monotone singer in church?) Music becomes beautiful when it has a melody, rising and falling of volume, tempo, and so on. This is true of everything in life.

The more life becomes the same—football teams running the same play every down, businesses that sell only one unchanging product for years, and so on—the more boring life becomes. This week I've talked to several people about Jesus. Some turned out to be believers, but in every case a variety of responses made the conversations rich. Let's face it, a lot of churches are pretty boring, in part because there is no variety—we know the drill. But when we are confronted with biblical truth that pushes us to change, even when it makes us uncomfortable, we see growth.

The Bible is rich in diversity: one central, unchanging message of redemption, one great story, but so filled with divergent characters, settings, times, and places. The Scriptures contain a host of genres, from narrative history to poetry and philosophy to commands. Begin to see uncertainty in witnessing as a beautiful part of God's work to grow and shape you as his child. If we can learn to see the uncertainties and fears of life as vital to our growth, we will change our perspective on the role of fear.

> Living for Jesus implies living a life of risk; it's time to start living!

Take a risk. It's funny how we take risks about things that don't matter. We will try a new food, workout, or outfit. We love to watch people who take risks on TV or on the Internet. But too many of us would rather be unhappy than uncertain; for the believer the steps of faith we take—though often uncertain in the moment—actually make us grow, which creates a more certain faith and joy. Living for Jesus implies living a life of risk; it's time to start living! My friend Al Gilbert says for people to be active sharing Christ, it's not *be taught then try*; it's *try then be taught*. I want you to try, to risk, and to see God working through you.

CHAPTER 2

God Is Not Mad at You: Understanding the Message

Now I would remind you, brothers, of the gospel I preached to you, which you received, in which you stand, and by which you are being saved, if you hold fast to the word I preached to you— unless you believed in vain. For I delivered to you as of first importance what I also received: that Christ died for our sins in accordance with the Scriptures, that he was buried, that he was raised on the third day in accordance with the Scriptures . . .

—1 Corinthians 15:1–4 ESV

The year: 1974, my freshman year in high school.

The class: English, my least favorite that year.

The book: Charles Dickens's *Great Expectations.*

The assignment: the one that filled my soul with terror, to give an oral report to my class.

My teacher: Mrs. Heard, a sweet, older African-American lady whose demeanor and pedagogy had nothing to do with the fear I recall from that class and that book. She simply

21

required each of us to do what freshmen students were asked to do across school districts then: to stand up in class and give an oral report on our reading. Sounds simple enough.

I was terrified. To this point in my educational journey, I'd done well in school. Now, for the first time I can remember, I refused to do an assignment. I sheepishly spoke to Mrs. Heard after class, telling her as respectfully as possible I would do anything, including taking a failing grade, but I simply could not stand up in front of the class to talk. I was sure if I did so I would either wet my pants or throw up (or both) out of sheer nerves.

I'd stood before my peers for spelling bees in elementary school. But my first year of high school brought an insecurity I had not known.

Fortunately, Mrs. Heard saw my terror as I begged her to let me skip the public report. She granted my request with a corresponding deduction in points (at that point I didn't care). I lived to see my sophomore year after all. If you had told me on that day I would spend my adult life talking to crowds of people, I would have moved to Tibet and become a Himalayan monk. I would do anything to keep from speaking in front of others.

That's how a lot of people feel when it comes to sharing Jesus with another person.

It could be how you feel.

I overcame my fears by God's grace. The desire to honor him eventually overcame my reticence, and the same can be true for you.

As a freshman I was expected to share the story of nineteenth-century England narrated by a man called Pip; you and I get to tell the story of the Savior of the world, the grand narrative of the God of all creation.

We aren't getting graded, because Jesus already passed the test, drank the cup, and made the way for us to know and glorify God.

We aren't getting judged, because Jesus already took the wrath of God for us.

We don't have to fear failing our Father in heaven, because we are his children, and no one loves their children like our Father loves us.

I feared my teacher getting angry with me. A lot of us fear God will be angry with us if we don't share our faith.

God is not mad at you. He loves you. Oh, he hates sin, no doubt about it. But Jesus bore our sin! Jesus also told us to keep his commands not out of fear of his wrath, but so that our joy would be made full (John 15:10–11 ESV).

Principle 2: In order to share Jesus confidently and consistently with others, first share him confidently and consistently with yourself.

A Gospel Vision

I want to tell you a story. It's a story that's not mainly about you, yet it has everything to do with you. It's similar to those you read in novels or enjoy in films, but it's a much greater story than these. It's the story that explains why you love all those other stories. It's a story that alone can make sense of your life and your place in this world. It's a story that makes sense of the joys and sorrows we face.

It's not just *a* story. It's *the* story, the one that frames all we know, dream, or need.

I'm talking about the gospel story.

The gospel, or good news, refers to the announcement of Jesus' triumph over sin by the cross and resurrection. It's also the story that explains this triumph through a grand narrative across all of Scripture. In Luke 24:44–48 and 1 Corinthians 15:1–4, we see first our Lord and then Paul tie the gospel reality of Jesus Christ dying for sinners and rising from the dead with all of Scripture. Read the passage in Luke:

> He told them, "These are my words that I spoke to you while I was still with you—that everything written about me in the Law of Moses, the Prophets, and the

Psalms must be fulfilled." Then he opened their minds to understand the Scriptures. He also said to them, "This is what is written: The Messiah would suffer and rise from the dead the third day, and repentance for forgiveness of sins would be proclaimed in his name to all the nations, beginning at Jerusalem. You are witnesses of these things."

In this passage you can see two ways we can understand the gospel. The first gets to the very heart of the gospel, the center of it all: the announcement of the death of Jesus, the sinless son of God, and His glorious resurrection for us (v. 46), and how, by repentance and faith, we can experience a new birth (v. 47). In the middle of our faith we have a bloody cross and a glorious resurrection! We read this repeatedly in places like Romans 5:8 and 2 Corinthians 5:21. The Gospel writers Matthew, Mark, Luke, and John unpack this in breathtaking detail.

Read again 1 Corinthians 15:1–4, quoted at the start of this chapter. Paul also shows us the gospel at its heart, or what I call the gospel in its *essence*: Christ died for our sins, was buried, and rose again (vv. 3–4).

While our gospel is not less than this, it is more, or what I call the gospel as *an epic story*. The entire Bible unpacks the larger, glorious story of the gospel. Look at these passages again. In Luke's passage, Jesus starts by explaining to the disciples *everything* in Moses, the Prophets, and the Psalms. What's he talking about? What we call the Old Testament. This was the Bible of the first century. Jesus demonstrates here how the gospel is central to the entire Bible, not just to the Gospel writers. And what about Paul's words in 1 Corinthians? Note how twice Paul says "according to the Scriptures"; that is, according to the Old Testament.

Most of us also have some knowledge of the whole biblical message and how the work of Christ relates to all Scripture. But most of the people with whom we have gospel conversations—and this is crucial—do not have such knowledge. They need to understand the gospel from the second way, from the perspective of the whole Bible. They need to see the story of Jesus is as big as the Bible itself, the story of Jesus is bigger than our times and our individual lives, or even the spiritual aspect of our lives alone.

We have a tendency today to make the gospel of Jesus more about what happens after we die than how we live today. Praise God it is about the afterlife! We have eternal hope. We have victory over death, hell, and the grave. But we also have hope in this life. The gospel changes us both eternally and daily.

The gospel is not only a message for the church to take to the world; it's a message for the church to take to heart personally. It's a message so big it takes the whole Bible to see it.

The Bible is amazing: sixty-six different books penned by a variety of writers over centuries. But all the thousands of stories in the various places involving myriads of people tell one great story in one expansive metanarrative, one overarching grand narrative: that God *created* a beautiful world, with humankind central to his great design; that sin came through the *fall* and has brought a world of brokenness; that God set apart a people through whom a *rescuer* would come, Jesus who redeems us through his death;

> The Bible has sixty-six books, but one great story of redemption.

and that we who come to God through repentance and faith have the hope of a *restoration*, where we will live in the very presence of God.

What Does Hollywood Have to Do with Calvary?

What's your all-time favorite movie? Think of just one.[8] Why do you love that movie? I've asked that question of thousands of teenagers and college students over the years. Young people love movies, after all (so do I). I get all kinds of examples, from

action movies (think *The Avengers* or *Star Wars*), to great epic
tales (*Lord of the Rings*), or romantic comedies. We love movies
and the stories they tell.

What if I told you the very reason novels grip us and movies move us is directly related to the grand gospel story of the
Bible? We live in a world that has lost the story of the Bible (and
many in the church have as well). I have found explaining the
gospel story helps unbelievers to see the big picture of God's
salvation, but it does more: it encourages believers to share this
great story with others. Missionaries overseas have done this a
long time with people who don't know the Word. We tend to
put the gospel in such overtly religious and ecclesiastical categories many lost people don't see its beauty and wonder.

Stories follow plotlines. I want to review three popular
storylines for you.[9] We see these in books and film again and
again, each told with its own nuances.

1. Man falls in a hole. This storyline (often called *Overcoming
the Monster*) starts off with the main character doing well, but
he falls in a hole of some sort, that is, he gets into a predica-
ment, he has some evil thing or person cause him distress, or
he finds himself in some other version of calamity. He cannot
save himself, so ultimately a rescuer comes to get him out of the
hole and back to well-being. Think of the *Die Hard* movies, any
of the Marvel films, or any other action adventure film. We love
stories that depict the evil and brokenness we see all around us,
but we love even more the rescue and restoration that follows.
Good storytellers take that simple storyline and rivet our attention and affections with how they tell it.

A version of this story is *Kill the Dragon, Get the Girl*, where
some evil creature or person wreaks terror among people but
at the end a hero kills the creature and rescues the damsel in
distress. My daughter, Hannah, and I loved the movie *Taken*
with Liam Neeson, which followed this storyline.

2. Boy meets girl. This is the classic romantic story, made
extremely popular in recent days with romantic comedies like

Hitch, The Proposal, Along Came Polly, and a host of other often-cheesy movies featuring actors like Ben Stiller, Will Smith, Adam Sandler, Will Ferrell, Jennifer Aniston, Sandra Bullock, and others. (I'm not endorsing them; just saying.) It includes romantic dramas such as *The Vow.*

There's a guy and a girl who somehow meet. A chemical reaction begins between them. Then you see two things depicted in these films. First, *guys are dumb.* Really dumb. The guy doesn't get the girl's hints, or does something dumb to hurt her feelings. They named a movie titled *Dumb and Dumber* about two guys, after all. Then you realize a second feature: *girls are crazy.* The girl overreacts, goes drama queen, and the movie continues with the two almost figuring things out, until the end when they actually do, and, to quote another movie in the genre, *Love Happens.*

3. Rags to riches. This is the story of *Cinderella,* or *The Princess Diaries,* or the favorite of Hannah's and mine from years ago, *What a Girl Wants.* Sadness ultimately leads to a rescue and restoration beyond the wildest dreams of the star of the story.

Why do I use these examples when talking about sharing the gospel? Matt Chandler, Josh Patterson, and Eric Geiger help us to see why through the eyes of two literary greats, C. S. Lewis and J. R. R. Tolkien:

> A conversation once held between colleagues C. S. Lewis and J. R. R. Tolkien speaks to this innate human desire for being part of larger-than-life stories, quests, and victories—the draw of our hearts toward "myths," which Lewis said were "lies and therefore worthless, even though breathed through silver."
>
> "No," Tolkien replied, "they are not lies." Far from being untrue, myths are the best way—sometimes the only way—of conveying truths that would otherwise remain inexpressible. We have come from God, Tolkien argued, and inevitably the myths woven by us,

though they do contain error, still reflect a splintered
fragment of the true light, the eternal truth that is with
God. Myths may be misguided, but they steer however
shakily toward the true harbor.[10]

These stories touch us because they speak to us, albeit
imperfectly, where the gospel has the power to change us, to
move our hearts toward the one who truly rescues and restores.
We want a life of joy. We know something has gone wrong. We
love and admire a rescuer, and we want a happily ever after,
a rescue and a restoration. These stories touch us because
they relate our lives to "the greatest epic the universe will ever
know—God reconciling all things to himself in Christ."[11]

You can see that sharing Christ is helpful when we relate
the gospel to truth we can see every day, whether in the stories
we love or the design we see. This is so vital for a culture that
no longer knows the story of the Bible. We don't need to choose
between the specific, propositional statements of gospel truth
and the glorious story of the Bible. But we do need to help
people see both the truth of the gospel and the great story of
God's redemptive plan.

My friends at Spread Truth Ministries (spreadtruth.com)
have developed a wonderful tool to help believers see the whole
gospel story of the Bible and share the good news of Jesus with
others. The booklet they created called *The Story* has been a
helpful tool for me.

Read more about *The Story* at viewthestory.com or down-
load the app.

A few years ago I began realizing in my own witness how
people I talked to didn't seem to get the point of the gospel.
It seemed more "churchy" to them than a message that would
impact all of their life. I wanted to help people—especially
young adults I interact with a lot—to see the great big picture
of God's plan and how their life related to God's glory. In
recent years I've seen more unchurched young adults come to

Christ through sharing the whole gospel story than with any other approach. The gospel story offers a guide to help explain the gospel based on where the person you are talking with is at the moment. I will be unpacking this throughout the book, but let me walk you through this here.

There are many wonderful tools and apps you can use to help you share Jesus more confidently. Unfortunately, sometimes evangelism training unintentionally focuses too much on doing the evangelism program just right, rather than really knowing the gospel so you can share it in a conversation.

If you are at a church that uses a certain tool, such as "The Gospel Journey" by Dare2Share Ministries,[12] "Two Ways to Live,"[13] any of the free tools from The Way of the Master Television,[14] or the courses offered by Christianity Explored,[15] for instance, the principles in this book can help you share Christ using any of these and more. I also use the *Life on Mission: 3 Circles*[16] conversation guide from the North American Mission Board (SBC). It's another way of using the gospel story through circles. I've often drawn the three circles on a napkin at a coffee shop, and earlier this month I led a young man to Christ doing just that. My friend Jimmy Scroggins first developed this excellent approach while reaching unchurched people in South Florida. I want you to learn the gospel is more than a tool, although tools that center on the gospel can help grow our gospel fluency. We all need a baseline of gospel understanding to have conversations about Jesus, and tools like these can help.

Knowing and Sharing the Gospel Story

When you put a puzzle together, you start with the border, since a framework makes the rest of the image make sense. The grand narrative of the Bible follows the plotline of creation, fall, rescue, and restoration, the framework of Scripture that "frames up" our world and our greatest need as well as God's

answer to that need: Jesus. This gives us foundational information that allows us to converse with others about him. Four key
words frame this grand story.

Creation

When starting conversations about Jesus, it helps to talk about
things we pretty much all agree on. It's easy for me to start with
creation because I love animals and the outdoors.

"It's a beautiful world, isn't it?" I've asked this question all
over the world: from Buddhist monks in Chiang Mai to young
men in Cape Town; from philosophy students at Aristotle
University in Greece to unchurched young adults in a Raleigh
restaurant. I've asked it of strangers on a plane and friends in
my neighborhood. To this point no one has disagreed with
me, because it *is* a beautiful world! This is obvious, coherent,
and real.

When you want to get away, where do you want to go? Not
to an office building. No, we all want to go to the mountains,
the beach, or the forest. It's refreshing. Why not talk with
people about that? It may lead to conversations about hunting,
fishing, photography, or a myriad of topics.

The gospel story doesn't begin in a manger. It begins
before the beginning, when God alone existed. Too often the
gospel is shared today almost like one more self-help plan.
Have you noticed one of the largest sections in a bookstore is
self-help? Books abound to help you remake yourself physically,
mentally, emotionally, relationally, financially, professionally,
and spiritually. Most of these have enough truth and practical
help to hook the reader, but most also miss the deepest issue
underlying our most fundamental need, to be reconciled with
our Creator. These books sell millions of copies but tend to
preach a false gospel of self-sufficiency and personal happi-
ness: "You can change your life, and we can help!"

We have to be careful not to make the gospel sound like
that. Panning the lens of our gospel understanding to a

Bible-wide view helps us to talk about Jesus in terms of all of life, not just our immediate situation or our spiritual lives alone. I've met too many unchurched and dechurched (formerly churched who chose to leave the church when becoming adults) who see the church as irrelevant to their spiritual quest because they see a less-than-grand view. We want people to see the love of Jesus is more boundless than the ocean, the glory of God more resplendent than the stars above, and being forgiven and restored to our heavenly Father

> The American Dream pales in comparison to the wonder of knowing our Creator.

more magnificent than any quick-fix attempt to make us happy. The American Dream pales in comparison to the wonder of knowing our Creator.

This is why the gospel story commences in Genesis 1 with God and the creation account. God—not you, not me—is the unequivocal center of the story. The Gospel of John, a treatise on salvation (see John 20:31), begins with creation as well. When Paul gave us a thorough explanation of the gospel and our salvation in the book of Romans, where did he start? Not with sin, though we tend to start at Romans 3:23. He starts with creation in Romans 1:20: "For his invisible attributes, that is, his eternal power and divine nature, have been clearly seen since the creation of the world."

God made a beautiful world, but he did something more. He made us unique, in his image (Gen 1:26–27). He gave us stewardship over the rest of creation and made us similar to but unlike anything else.

As I continue my conversation with my unbelieving friend, I mention how we as people are unique in all of nature. Again, no one has disagreed with me on this. We are different rationally. Ants build a hill and bees a hive; beavers make a dam and birds build nests. But we build cities, space stations, and cell phones, and discover the Internet. We also ask questions, like "Why?"

We differ artistically. Birds sing songs; we write symphonies. We build museums and create all forms of art.

We differ in our roles. We exercise stewardship over creation, as noted above. We work with a purpose. (Work came before the fall, by the way.) We were given the mission to be fruitful and multiply and fill the earth for a greater purpose: to worship the God who made us.

We alone were made to worship and obey the one true God. Everyone worships. Some worship their intellect or a variety of idols, but make no mistake, we all worship. As the church father Augustine said in a prayer: "You made us for yourself, and our hearts are restless until they rest in you."

We have an insatiable appetite to find purpose, to live a life that matters. God built that into each of us. We want to live for something bigger.

Fall

As I talk with people about our beautiful world and our uniqueness, I then ask, "But something has gone wrong in our world, hasn't it?" It's pretty easy to talk about the obvious brokenness all around us; it's a part of everyone's life. Talking of sin by starting with the brokenness we see all around us and moving to its personal effects keeps people from becoming defensive with the "oh, no, one more Christian telling me I'm a sinner" look. Often the person with whom I'm talking will bring up examples of brokenness in a conversation. Death, disease, and all sorts of turmoil in the world are easy to see.

As we talk about brokenness and sin, we should become very vulnerable, describing the struggles we have and still face. I may talk about my artificial hip and back issues, or how I've been diagnosed with attention deficit disorder, which can be annoying. We all have struggles, and it's vital we Christians not sound like we have everything together and we have become sinless. We are forgiven; we are not flawless.

I explain how sin has affected everything. Sin is not a collection of our mistakes; it's the very reality that we are in rebellion toward God and cannot save ourselves (Rom 3:10–23).
When I'm talking with someone, I relate this to young children:
no parent has ever had to teach a child to disobey, right? We
have to teach children to obey, as disobedience is in our very
nature. Think of anything noble you have sought to do. You've
never met a person who perfectly stuck to a diet, or a workout
regimen, or who gave 100 percent of their best to every single
assignment in school forever. We all have a slacker tendency
built in to us. "Prone to wander, Lord, I feel it, / Prone to leave
the God I love," as the hymn says.[17]

Because of sin, we are in rebellion to God, facing eternity
separated from him in hell. We were created for glory, but we
stand in judgment. This is the not-good news people must see
to embrace the beauty of the good news in the cross.

Rescue

After talking about this, I like to say, this is why Jesus came: not
mainly to get us to curse less or lust less, or to get us to attend
church more regularly. These are some of the effects of the
gospel, and many in and out of the church have confused the
essence of the gospel with its
effects. Too many times people see
Christianity as a group of religious
people trying to impose their
moral code on them. They know
what we are against. We excel at
articulating that. But, we don't

> Many in and out of the
> church have confused
> the essence of the
> gospel with its effects.

want people we meet to see Christianity as mainly a moral code
to follow. Jesus condemned the Pharisees for that approach to
serving God. It's true when we meet Jesus our behavior is
changed. But that's not all. Paul tells us in 2 Corinthians 5:16–
17 we are totally remade, a new creation, when we are saved. We

see the world differently, and we respond like Christ; an aspect of that is our moral change.

What if people who don't know Christ who know Christians saw us less as moral police, and more like Joseph, who was imprisoned for no crime, and yet continued to walk with God through his years in jail until he became second to Pharaoh? Joseph had a different perspective, that God intended his life ultimately to bring good (Gen 50:20). What if we imitated Paul who was imprisoned for preaching the gospel? Chained to a soldier, Paul considered the soldier chained to him, and rejoiced he had a captive audience to talk about Jesus. How could Paul rejoice even while being in prison (see Phil 1)? Paul certainly talked about moral change, but he always did so out of the context of larger gospel change, and that change included everything—spiritually, relationally, emotionally, financially, physically, and morally—all aspects of our life are changed by the gospel.

A powerful, recent demonstration of the gospel's power to bring change came in 2015, but not from a famous evangelist or a megachurch pastor. It came from family members in a small African-American church in Charleston, South Carolina. Dylann Roof shot to death nine people in a racially incited massacre. But when relatives spoke to Roof at his court appearance, they spoke of forgiveness and called on him to turn to Christ. "I forgive you," Nadine Collier, daughter of a victim, said. "I forgive," added another, who stated, "Give your life to the one who matters most: Christ."[18] People need to hear the message of the gospel; they also need to see its remarkable change.

> Jesus Christ didn't come to make bad people good, but to make dead people live!

As I talk to a lot of people who in their minds have been burned by the church and are interested in spiritual things but wary of the church, I want to be clear in explaining the wonderful grace of Jesus that changes our perspective on everything. The essence of the gospel is something far greater than behavior modification. Jesus Christ didn't come to make bad people good, but to make dead people live! I have met too many who don't understand grace, God's unmerited favor toward us through Christ.

When I'm sharing Jesus I explain some of the terms describing what Christ has done. You and I were guilty before the judgment bar of the righteous God, but by Jesus' death we are declared justified, or not guilty. We owed a debt from sin we could never pay, but Jesus both paid the penalty for our sin debt and offers us an inheritance we could never earn, called reconciliation. We who were slaves to sin have been set free from slavery: we've been redeemed, a slave market term. I could speak of so much more, of salvation, and adoption, and a new birth.

Just now, typing these words, I want to tell someone about my Savior! Do you see how preaching this to ourselves regularly can help us to share it with others effectively?

Just like how we love it when the hero in a movie rescues those in danger, we love the thought of being delivered from sin. All those storylines I mentioned above are reflected in the work of Christ. We are in a hole; only Jesus can get us out. We seek a relationship that lasts with one who loves us perfectly, and Jesus is the One. We are all in rags, paupers wrecked by sin, but Jesus will give us the riches of glory by faith.

Remember "Kill the dragon, get the girl"? Jesus defeated the works of the devil, that old dragon, on the cross. One day, he will present the bride of Christ, his church, at the wedding feast of the lamb. Kill the dragon, get the girl.

Restoration

The reason we love stories with a happily ever after, and the reason Hollywood makes movie after movie with this ending, is because we all yearn for this. Most young people today don't think a lot daily about the afterlife, but we all want our lives to matter. And when we do think about forever, we want it to be a happy ever after. God has prepared a place for those who love him that is beyond our ability to comprehend. We are stuck with human language, so the best we can say is it has streets of gold. It's so much grander than that.

Jesus is going to return one day and take his bride, all believers, to a new heaven and earth. We will be in the very presence of Jesus, the one who saved us and walks with us. Take hope in that fact.

In the meantime, we walk on this earth with a commission to take this glorious good news to others. It's a blessing more than a burden, and the more we see how great our salvation is in Christ, the more this becomes obvious.

In June, about three months ago as I write this, I had the opportunity to meet a server in a local restaurant. As I had lunch with Michelle and some of our young professionals from church, I asked Mary[19] if we could pray for her as we prayed for her meal. This led to further conversation where she admitted she was trying to sort out just what she believed. She agreed to meet with me along with some young pros at a local café. I simply walked through this gospel story, and she trusted Christ! She had little church background and knew next to nothing about the Bible, but the story of the gospel made sense and described the longing of her heart.

If you are new at this and sharing Christ has not been a part of your lifestyle, it's okay to take baby steps. You can order a gospel booklet like *The Story* from the website noted previously, or the *3 Circles* from namb.net. Simply give the booklet to another person and say something like this: "This is a little Bible study that explains in a few pages the story of the whole Bible. Look it over and let's talk about it soon." Leave it with them, and pray for God to use that. Don't say, "Read this tract, you heathen." I've seen believers lead someone to Christ for the first time by starting with a booklet like this.

Living the Story with God at the Center

A reason a lot of us don't talk about Jesus to others is we have been too overburdened by moralism to be amazed at his glorious riches and grace. Knowing Jesus changes our eternal destiny: we no longer have to fear death. Knowing Jesus also impacts every aspect of our lives. Study the New Testament to grow in your understanding of this. Read Paul's epistles and watch for times he applies the reality of knowing Christ to everything from finances (see 2 Cor 8–9) to overcoming temptation (see 1 Cor 6:18–20), to marriage (Eph 5), and so much more.

Before you started reading this book you had already determined what you value most, what brings you joy, what stirs your sense of justice, what you would fight to protect, and what you love to talk about. How central is your heavenly Father to the core of your values?

Tim Chester and Steve Timmis offer a beautiful and encouraging summary of how to think about God and our relationship with God and others because of salvation. Here is what they say in summary:[20]

1. *God is great, so we don't have to be in control.* We are all control freaks, so admit it. God is sovereign. He has the power to save.
2. *God is glorious, so we don't have to fear others.* We are also at some level all people pleasers and struggle with the fear of man. Learning to please God alone is crucial to our spiritual growth. He is glorious. Fear him, not man.
3. *God is good, so we don't have to look elsewhere.* Temptation can be powerful, but when we sin we are saying in that moment we don't believe God is good enough.
4. *God is gracious, so we don't have to prove ourselves.* We have been forgiven completely by the one we have offended

immensely. Enjoy the grace of God lavished on us through Christ.

These statements have been profound in my life. I review them regularly. In order for Jesus to move from our lives through our lips to others, he must reign in our hearts.

{ CHAPTER 3 }

It's Easier than You Think: Conversations, Not Presentations

So he reasoned in the synagogue with the Jews and with those who worshiped God, as well as in the marketplace every day with those who happened to be there.

—Acts 17:17

The aroma of fresh-ground coffee can't be missed: dark roast, espresso beans, and fresh lattes, all robust and alluring, filling the air. The sound of smooth music lingers in the background. Throw in a corner table, add in a friend, and curl your fingers around your favorite cup of joe, and what do you get?

I call that a great place for conversation.

"But I'm not a coffee drinker," you protest. Here's another venue I like: Cracker Barrel, sitting across from Michelle, ordering breakfast for supper, and talking about life. Sound inviting?

Maybe you picture fishing on a bass boat with a friend or in a deer stand with a hunting buddy. Perhaps you'd stop for a bite at Panera after shopping at the mall.

We could come up with endless examples of places we enjoy talking to others. Whether we are extroverts (raising my hand) or introverts (like a lot of really normal people), we all love conversations with friends.

Over the past few years I've seen a transition from giving a gospel presentation to having gospel conversations. I've also seen a transition in my own life and witness from focusing on a night a week of visitation to a deliberate emphasis on meeting people at "third places" (like coffee shops). I still go on visitation night at our church at times, like this week in fact, but increasingly my witness has transitioned from that as a focus to everyday conversations both planned and unexpected.

I fear people like me who want to help people like you learn to share Christ with normal people like us sometimes set you up for failure before you start. We stress you out over getting the information right, or we only give examples of someone being gloriously converted when we shared with them, to the neglect of talking about conversations where people don't trust Christ immediately, or we overburden you with details to the point that you are pretty wigged out before you start.

> A big reason we don't talk to unbelievers about Jesus is because we don't talk to one another about Jesus.

What if you could just talk about Jesus to others simply because you love him and you love them and you want to introduce them to him?

What if we spent less time giving people scripted evangelistic presentations and instead simply learned to introduce Jesus into the normal conversations we already have?

What if I told you that the gospel you received and the life God gave you are all you need to start having real, effective conversations with people about Jesus?

A big reason we don't talk to unbelievers about Jesus is because we don't talk to one another about Jesus. What if talking about Jesus were not awkward, but became as normal as talking about other things we enjoy?

Principle 3: Shifting from giving an evangelistic presentation to having an evangelistic conversation takes pressure off the witness and relates the gospel more clearly to an unbeliever.

Connecting People to Jesus

In the last chapter I overviewed the gospel, emphasizing the glory of the gospel story of God's work from creation to our redemption. I hope you've begun "preaching" that to yourself, going over it again and again, to encourage yourself.

What if you stepped beyond telling yourself this good news and chatted with a friend this week about Jesus? Suppose you took a risk and found yourself, during a conversation, talking with her about your Savior. And suppose at the end of the conversation she remarked how she wished she had the relationship with God she sees in you. You find yourself saying, "You can have that relationship because of Jesus."

Then she does the unthinkable. She ways, "I want that."

Cue the party music. This doesn't occur every time we talk about Jesus. It doesn't happen most of the time. But it does happen, and when it does you don't need to hesitate to encourage them to follow Jesus.

What do we do when we tell someone about Jesus and they wish to be saved? I've often asked the following questions after sharing the gospel with someone:[21]

- "Does what we have been discussing make sense to you?"

- "Is there any good reason why you would not be willing to receive God's gift of eternal life?"
- "Are you willing to turn from your sin and place your faith in Jesus right now?"

Explain the commitment she is to make. Remind her that Christianity is a relationship, not a ritual.

If she says yes to the final question, here's a simple process to help her. First, pray *for* her, thanking God for bringing you together, for the wonder of salvation, and the work of the Spirit. Second, pray *with* her, helping her as needed to cry out to God for salvation. You can pray with her, having her repeat after you. You can have her pray in her own words. You can invite her to pray silently. Just a couple weeks ago I had the honor of leading a lady to Christ whom I met with a friend at a coffee shop. She prayed silently, although in my experience I typically guide someone with a prayer.

Finally, ask her to thank God for what he has done through Christ, and then you thank God as well. I've heard some wonderful prayers of gratitude on occasions like this.

The Scriptures do not give a prescribed "sinner's prayer," so a formula isn't required. However, the Bible does encourage a lost person to cry out to God for salvation (Rom 10:9, 13); so encouraging someone to pray to God for salvation can be deduced from Scripture.

When you have the opportunity to lead someone to Christ you will want to help them grow. Since the Bible calls a new believer a child in the faith, I use the idea of family to show the basics for a new believer:

- *Food:* a child needs food; we feed on the Word.
- *Family:* a child of God has a new family in the local church; baptism relates to this.
- *Air:* a child needs to breathe; prayer becomes the way to connect with God.

- *Purpose:* every child needs a purpose; ours is to glorify God, and a vital way to do so is to bring more children to God through sharing this good news with others.

I often ask about two people: who does she know who would be *happy* to hear of her desire to follow Christ? And, who *needs* to know this as well? Go tell them, I say!

Many believers freak out thinking about this for a simple reason: you've never seen anyone led to Christ by another believer. You can see two examples of the gospel being shared and someone being led to Christ here: bhacademic.com/sharingjesus.

Be patient with a new believer when he follows Christ. Years ago a friend remarked how some people are saved like the stinging of a bee: a sudden, dramatic change. Others seem to blossom like a flower: there is a new birth, but the change comes more slowly over time. A person is changed when they meet Jesus, but people demonstrate that change differently. He is a spiritual baby, so patiently help him to grow.

Gospel Presentation or Conversation?

Our day of increasing biblical illiteracy calls us to move from giving a rigid gospel *presentation* to having gospel *conversations*. This means we develop a certain amount of "gospel intelligence"[22] or "gospel fluency"[23] so we can introduce the good news in everyday discussions.

Both presentations and gospel conversations have their place. Some people know enough gospel content to be reached through a simple presentation. If someone walks up to you and asks how to be saved, just lay out the gospel for him. I'm not hating on learned presentations, but I'm arguing that, increasingly in our world, presentations are less effective and conversations connect better, especially with the younger generation. Some differences:

Presentation	Conversation
Starts in our Christian worldview	Starts in the other person's worldview
Assumes they have some knowledge of the gospel	Assumes they don't know the gospel
Focuses on the lost person as a sinner	Focuses on the *imago Dei* in the sinner
Effective with people with a church background	Effective regardless of church background
Focuses on immediate decision	Hopes for a decision but appreciates the process involved in reaching people today

When I first learned how to share my faith, I learned a simple technique to move from a casual encounter to a gospel presentation: ask leading questions that let you jump right into the gospel message. I'm grateful for this as I've seen many come to Christ this way. But for increasing numbers of unbelievers in America, virtually interrupting them to share a gospel presentation does not come as easily as it did thirty years ago. Today, evangelistic conversations matter more than ever.

In a gospel conversation the witness seeks to do more than get an unbeliever's attention enough to present the gospel to them. It seeks to do more than share the gospel as briefly as possible with people we hardly know; it starts in the worldview of the unbeliever, shows them truth they already affirm, and then moves from that truth to show the gospel, as Paul did in Athens in Acts 17, starting with an unknown god and with creation. Or, as Peter did in Acts 2 with devout Jews, starting with the Old Testament and emphasizing Jesus as Messiah.

Different approaches; same gospel. Different audiences; same message.

I live in the Raleigh-Durham area, one of the fastest growing and more progressive cities in America. I spend a lot of time talking with young adults (we call them young pros, or young professionals, at church) who are either unchurched or dechurched. The shift from monologic evangelistic presentations (I talk, you listen) to dialogical conversations (we talk together and listen to one another) has been crucial for my witness, and I'm learning this is true for many I meet who minister in the increasingly post-Christian America of today.

You don't have to be an amazingly skilled speaker or have remarkable presentation skills. You simply have to engage in conversations, something we do daily. If you read the book of Acts, you will find a few people were called to preach to crowds. People like Peter, Paul, and Barnabas. But ordinary believers had conversations with others, telling people they met the good news they found in Christ (see Acts 2:10–11; 4:29–31; 8:1–4; and 11:19–22).

Just this week I used movies and plotlines to show a server in Waffle House the gospel. She already believed movies have a storyline that often value a rescue, and she definitely loves movies with a happy ending and wants one for her life. From there I showed her the biblical plotline, and it made perfect sense to her. I have led more unchurched people to Christ in the last three years starting in their worldview like this than I have trying to get them to begin by agreeing with mine.

I led a young lady named Allie to Christ by talking with her about how beautiful the world that God designed is, and how everything around us has such harmony. She totally agreed. I then observed how something has gone wrong, and how people struggle with brokenness—including everything from natural disasters and disease to personal choices and circumstances. She agreed, and we conversed for some time about this. Then, I showed her how Jesus came not to get her to church services or to make her toe the line of a moral code, but to rescue people, including her, from the brokenness in the world caused by sin. She totally saw this and immediately followed Christ.

Helping you learn to have conversations with your unsaved friends takes the pressure off of you learning a presentation you must recite with precision. We have conversations all the time, every day. We need to stop putting evangelism in a different category than just talking to people. I love what Tim Chester and Steve Timmis say: we need to have "ordinary people doing ordinary things with gospel intentionality."[24]

Conversations Are Relaxing, Presentations Can Be Unnerving

My friend Jim Gillespie likes to say "Every conversation is a ministry opportunity." What if we saw conversations that way? In our everyday conversations, various ideas about God and spirituality often come up. We can learn to steer conversations to Christ. We see Jesus do this with the Samaritan woman in John 4. When we focus our conversations on the worldview of those around us, we can become less preoccupied with our presentation and more focused on them. We can learn how to naturally help people see how their personal story relates to God's greater story seen in Scripture.

> Every conversation is a ministry opportunity.
> —Jim Gillespie

As boys, my brother and I had an aquarium with tropical fish. If we got a new aquarium, took it home, filled it up, and then simply released our new exotic fish into the water from their bags of water from the store, what would happen? We would soon have a ceremony around the toilet as we said goodbye to our now-dead fish. No, we first had to prepare the water in the tank, removing the chlorine, adjusting the temperature, and let them sit in the aquarium in their bag of water for a time until we released them. Our goal was not to dump in the fish as quickly as possible, but to have an aquarium full of fish for a long time. In the same way, our goal must not be to dunk people into the living water of the gospel as fast as we can, but to show them the wonder of the living water that alone can quench their deepest thirst. We want to help folks see that living in their current bag of water does not compare to the ocean of life Christ gives.

I'm not discouraging you from leading someone to Christ the first time you share with them. I have seen this often myself. But for most—especially if we really want to reach the masses of people who have no understanding of Christ, the people we are not currently reaching—we want to take them on a journey, led by the Spirit, empowered by the gospel, to meet their Creator. This happens through gospel conversations, and often through a series of conversations over a period of time.

As I've taught this in recent days in my classes at Southeastern Baptist Theological Seminary and to laity in our church, I've had several tell me that as they were talking with someone, they suddenly realized they were conversing about Jesus without trying to give a set presentation. In each case they told me how this approach took a lot of pressure off them as they shared the good news. It seemed more natural, more real.

Connecting People's Passion or Pain to Christ

Take a moment and think about a specific conversation you had this week with a coworker, neighbor, or friend. More than likely, in the course of the conversation they either brought up some concern or they talked about a hope or dream.

Over the next few days listen to the things people you meet talk about. We converse regularly—either in serious conversations or in casual chitchat—about our *pain* or our *passion*.[25] In such conversations we can easily talk about Christ.

I fly a lot. I recently got on an airplane and took my typical aisle seat, this time in the very back row. A young lady named

Alex who was carrying a bag full of tennis rackets sat next to me. A lot of my trips have collegiate athletes on them because of all the universities in our area. She told me she was a freshman at a major college in the Midwest, returning home from a tennis tournament. We chatted a bit; I told her I was a professor and a minister who worked with young people like her. She told me her major was communication, focusing on using technology to communicate information. I asked her a question I love to ask young people, "If you were not limited by money or geography, where would you go and what would you do?"

She replied immediately. "I'd work for Pixar," she said with a smile.

"Why Pixar?" I asked.

"They are the best!" she replied.

We had a natural, not forced, conversation, moving from her passion for excellence in her career (I shared a similar passion for teaching) to the gospel. She grew up in church and admitted to losing her focus on spiritual things after arriving at college. I told her she was pathetic and had to get right with God or she would burn. Okay, I didn't exactly say those words, although I urged her to yield all her life to Jesus. She didn't trust Christ, but she admitted her need and thanked me for taking time to help her see how she had lost her way. One of the simplest ways to introduce Jesus naturally in a conversation grows out of talking about one's passion.

Similarly, I spoke through a pastor who served as my interpreter to young men in the settlements of Cape Town, South Africa. You could see the brokenness in the razor wire and walled-in homes. These young men spoke of the brokenness in their community from drugs and crime. We talked about how no one wants to raise a family in those conditions, and how such brokenness makes us seek a better way. From the brokenness we discussed I moved from the effects of sin back to God's plan in creation, and how Jesus' work on the cross could change them to see a more beautiful world and have hope for a better world in the resurrection. I'm sure it was through the more excellent interpretation of the pastor, but all seven of those young men trusted Christ that day. In a conversation we were able to give context to the brokenness around them and hope beyond their circumstances. That's what the gospel can do.

A Gospel Conversation: You Can Do This

Sharing Christ conversationally makes sense when we remember three vital things people can tell about us in a conversation:

1. People can tell if you *care* about them. They don't care how much you know about God until they know how much you care about them.
2. People can tell if you *believe* what you are talking about. We will not convince every person we meet who does not know Jesus that they must believe in him, but let them not doubt that we believe.
3. People can tell if the *hand of God is on your life*. There is something very powerful about a simple, honest conversation about Jesus. Our lives and our lips testify to our faith.

Matt Carter, pastor of the Austin Stone Community Church in Austin, Texas, told me about a friend he had in high school. Matt was quite a rebellious young man when he met Jesus at age eighteen. His friend immediately dropped their relationship. He was uninterested in this new Jesus Freak Matt had become. Years later Matt discovered this friend now lived in Austin. Matt prayed that God would help him find this friend. The next day (no kidding) an elder in his church texted him to say he was at a dinner party and this guy (Matt's old friend) was there. He got Matt the man's number and they reconnected.

Matt took him to dinner. They caught up about life, and his friend asked Matt about his church and his life. Matt gave his testimony, just like we talked about in chapter 2. When

Matt looked at his friend and simply said, "Jesus changed my life, and gave me peace I had never experienced," the friend broke into tears. "I so want to have peace," he said. At the time of writing this he has not trusted Christ, but he is very open to talking more about this with Matt.

If Jesus is the greatest thing that ever happened to us, he should come up in conversations. Not forced, not structured, but simply because he is the biggest deal in our lives.

Having Conversations That Include the Gospel

Over the last forty years more Christians in America have learned an evangelistic presentation than ever in history, because more evangelism training programs have been developed and taught than ever before. That's not a bad thing; when I learned to share Christ using the tract *The Four Spiritual Laws,* I soon led someone to Christ for the first time. We have to honestly ask the question, though, if training multitudes of believers has been as effective as we would have hoped. Pastors tell me most of those who have learned the presentations pretty much never actually share them as a lifestyle. In my tradition, the Southern Baptist Convention, training has been a central part of our world, but baptisms have declined for a generation.

Let's face it—it's easier to set a group of believers at a church in one room to learn one outline and one plan. But to mature disciples, our goal is to help every follower of Christ to learn to live for him—including sharing him with others—in a way that fits the gifts and abilities of each person. Our goal in training is not to get people to learn a technique but to be confident in sharing Jesus naturally and organically because they can't help but share him.

Most times your conversation will not lead to a conversion but will help nudge the person further along in their gospel understanding. It's comforting to know that we are part of a bigger work of the Holy Spirit in the lives of those we meet. "As often as not, our role is to move people one or two steps along the way rather than get them all the way to number ten in one go," Chester and Timmis note. They add: "Trust him to take the little morsel of the gospel message you give to people and use it as part of his purposes in their life."[26]

I pray you will move from focusing on getting every word just right in a presentation to knowing the gospel's reality in your own life, leading you to have regular conversations with people in which you increasingly talk about Christ with growing confidence. We have conversations all the time, and as believers we have some pretty amazing good news to converse about.

No matter how conversational we become, our conversations about Christ will sometimes become uncomfortable. The gospel, no matter how winsomely we share it, confronts us at our very core. Our conviction of its truth should always outweigh the discomfort of hard conversations. I had the opportunity years ago to share Christ in Salt Lake City with Mormons at Temple Square. As I spoke to a young missionary, I shared Christ with her. She resisted the message, insisting on her experience with Mormonism as sufficient. It was honestly hard to look at this kind coed and explain to her the jeopardy she faced by not trusting the Jesus proclaimed in the New Testament. As graciously as possible, I warned her of judgment and the reality of hell, knowing the god of this world had blinded her mind (see 2 Cor 4:4). It was disheartening in that moment to see her reject Christ, as I knew I would likely never see her again. We speak the truth with grace, regardless of the response. Even when we have to have hard conversations, we can help those with whom we share to understand the importance of Christ, the reality of hell, and the hope of the gospel more effectively by conversations than through rote presentations.

CHAPTER 4

It's Not in Your Power, yet You Are Vital

From one man he has made every nationality to live over the whole earth and has determined their appointed times and the boundaries of where they live.

—Acts 17:26

If I'd been born a century earlier, I would've been dead by age forty. Which would've made it pretty hard to write something. Which means you wouldn't be reading this book. Why? I broke my hip in 1996 at age thirty-seven. Before more recent surgical advances, this broken hip would have developed gangrene, leading to an excruciating death within a few years. The medical advancement of an artificial hip replacement gave me a new lease on life.

I love technology.

How would we make it without Google today? How would life be without microwaves, flat-screen TVs, or smartphones? Today there are more cell phones on the earth than people. I can hop on a plane and be halfway around the world in a day, and then talk to you face-to-face from the other side of the globe via the Internet.

It's a truly remarkable time to be alive. It's also remarkable how you had no control over when and where you were born.

There is so much over which you have no control:

- Who your parents are
- Your eye color
- Your ethnicity
- Your height (heels don't count)
- Your personality, such as whether you are an introvert or extrovert

There is so much more. You and I do control a lot: our weight, for instance. Okay, even our weight involves genetic factors beyond us. Genetics load the gun of our health, but our lifestyle pulls the trigger.[27] We definitely control our passion, who we count as our friends, and lots of daily choices (like what we eat).

You're reading a book about sharing Jesus, but you could have been born in a land where you would never have received the education that allows you to read. You could have been born, lived, and died without ever hearing of Jesus. And yet here you are, at this time and place in history, with all your gifts, talents, passions, opportunities, and even your limitations in front of you.

It's a Great Time to Live, to Love, and to Share Jesus

Christians once had the home-field advantage in the West: even people who didn't believe in Jesus had some general idea of the message, some awareness of who God is, and an understanding of right and wrong based generally on Scripture. We don't live in that world anymore. That's why it's a great time to share Jesus. Why do I say that?

Our post-Christian world today resembles the pre-Christian world of the New Testament, when the gospel spread like a wildfire across the Roman Empire. Believers proclaimed an unchanging message, but how they shared it varied based on their audience. In Acts 2, all the believers shared the mighty work of God (vv. 10–11). Peter stood up to proclaim the gospel to the crowd, and what did he do? He quoted the Old Testament, the Hebrew Bible. He explained how Jesus was the Messiah the Jews sought. And why did Peter do that? His audience consisted of devout Jews who had assembled in Jerusalem from all over the Roman Empire for Pentecost. They had a common belief system, a knowledge of and belief in the Hebrew Scriptures, and a common desire. Peter showed them Jesus was the fulfillment of God's Word, and three thousand believed that day.

Fast forward to Acts 17. In the latter half of that chapter we read of Paul in Athens. He seized an opportunity to speak to Athenians at Mars Hill. Unlike Peter in Jerusalem, Paul didn't quote the Old Testament, nor did he refer to Jesus as the Messiah. He started with creation, found common ground, and took his listeners to the cross and resurrection.

I grew up in an America like Jerusalem in Acts 2: most people had some notion of biblical teaching and the God of Scripture, even if they rejected it. Today, we live in Athens, in a land without a biblical mind or a biblical grounding in who God is or how we can know him. Many if not most Americans, and people globally, start from a different place than a biblical vantage point as they live their lives.

The gospel has not changed, but how we share it does change. We can't make the assumptions about people that we once did, like that they have some idea of the Bible in general or the gospel specifically. We can more likely assume people think being a Christian means doing more good things than bad, which is moralism, not the gospel. That's why we have to engage people in conversations and show them how the whole gospel story relates to their stories, and how God's work in Christ to rescue us is the key, not our works. What a great time to introduce people to the story that makes sense of our messed-up world.

There's a fascinating verse in Paul's message at Mars Hill, which I quoted at the start of this chapter, that relates not only to unbelievers but also to us. See what he says in verse 26? God determined your appointed time and the boundaries of where you live.

You could have been born a thousand years ago.

In Tibet. Or Australia.

You could have been, but you weren't. Well, not a thousand years ago anyway. You could be from Australia.

There's a lot about you that you can't control. There's also something very wrong with you and me that only Jesus can fix. This is why the two most important days of your life are the day you were born and the day you figure out why you were born. You had no control over the circumstances of your physical birth, but through the second birth, salvation in Jesus, you discover the why!

Principle 4: God has sovereignly placed you in this world at this time with the abilities and gifts you have to bring glory to him and show the joy of the gospel to others.

Theologically, God put you here when he did, in the way he made you, with the circumstances in your life for a purpose much bigger than you, and the very drive you have for your life to matter comes from him. But as we have sinned and screwed things up royally, God alone can fix what is wrecked in us. That's why the cross and resurrection matter so much.

You and I don't choose the meaning of life. Greg Forster observes some things we choose and some we don't:

> You do get to decide how best to respond to the circumstances and conditions life presents you with, and that kind of personal liberty is a good thing. But you

don't get to decide what the circumstances and conditions of your life will be, and those unchosen circumstances and conditions—including relationships and obligations—are a central part of who you are. To a large extent, they determine the scope and significance of choices that you will have the freedom to make.[28]

Learning what you control and what you don't helps your witness. The more you see how God wired you uniquely, the more you can learn how to live for him—including talking to others about him—in the way he created you to, uniquely, for his glory and your good. There are things God has put in your life over which you have no control, which are gifts from God.

This is why a one-size-fits-all evangelism program is less vital than developing gospel fluency, where you learn to speak about Jesus out of your personality with the strengths and the limitations with which God has blessed you. This also roots your witnessing in your overall growth as a believer. When you choose wisely regarding those things over which you have control, it affects all your life, including your witness. We choose whether or not we will exercise our bodies with a bike ride or exercise our minds with a good book. We choose whether or not we will read our Bibles or pray, share our faith or participate in our local church.

Start with Why, Not How

Your current practice of witnessing or lack of it is not the issue. It's a symptom of your growth in Christ in general. Our witness provides a strong barometer of our overall discipleship. Have you ever gone on a diet to lose weight and gained it all back about as fast as you lost it? Me too. Why is that? We tend to treat the symptom, not the issue underneath. We don't need to go on a diet to become healthy; statistically speaking, diet plans fail at a remarkable rate. Instead, we need to develop a lifestyle of healthy eating habits. Did you get the key word? *Habit.*

In his excellent book *Start with Why,* author Simon Sinek explains how successful leaders don't focus on *how* to do something as much as *why.*[29] I'm afraid a lot of Christians want to learn how to share their faith or pray without really understanding *why.* Sharing Christ starts with understanding God's grand story, centering on Christ, and includes his creation of you to know him and to bring him glory. That's the big *why.*

Your *why* is not to do things to keep God from being angry with you, or to impress your friends with your spiritual prowess. For your Christianity to be bigger than you, your *why* has to be as big as God. Paul's *why* was to know Christ and to make him known (see Phil 3); this explains the *how* of him rejoicing in Christ even while being in jail for his faith. His *why* was big enough to face persecution with joy. I'm afraid the *why* of many American believers won't get us to talk to our neighbors about Jesus, let alone prepare us to face persecution.

> For your Christianity to be bigger than you, your *why* has to be as big as God.

You live your *why* practically as you develop habits that fit you, your personality, and your lifestyle, to help you live out the gospel as God wired you to do. That's the *how.*

Why comes before *how* in all of life. When I hit age fifty and got my annual physical, I realized I was at least forty pounds overweight. I had developed excuses as to *why* it wasn't my fault. I have an artificial hip, remember? I can't run. I'm over half a century old. I travel a lot and eat out all the time. I have a sedentary job; on and on I could go.

I knew this was baloney. My body is the temple of the Holy Spirit. I want to take care of it, and I want to be able to teach and preach and write when I'm eighty. God began to change my *why*. My motivation had less to do with my appearance—looking younger, for instance—and more to do with being able to serve Jesus well into my eighties. When my *why* grew out of a desire to glorify God, I started to lose weight and get healthier.

Once I changed my *why*, then I could change my habits. I did a variety of fitness regimens. I also had to change my diet, which was hard. I went through a couple of years with some serious back issues that caused me to refine my *why* and refocus my habits. Today I am in my later fifties, over forty pounds lighter than I was at fifty, and although I still have a metal hip and some very real lumbar spine issues, I'm in many ways healthier than I have been in decades.

I had to get the correct *why*; I then had to develop habits that not only helped me live out the *why*, but that also fit me personally with my own strengths and limitations.

It's the same with your witness. If you don't come to understand the depth of God's love for you, the amazing grace in the redemption you have in Christ, and the wonder that God has wired you for his purposes—the big *why*—no technique in witnessing will change you. But if you get all this, you still need practical habits that fit you and create a lifestyle where showing and sharing Christ becomes as much a part of you as the diet you eat and the clothing style you wear.

Throughout this book I relate your witness to your fitness (not just because it rhymes, either), and your spiritual life to other aspects of life. For too long we've compartmentalized our spiritual lives into a completely separate category for church and church-type activities. Doing this has not helped our witness, and it has done something else: it's made it seem as if the "real" spiritual people are those who are called to vocational ministry, like pastors, foreign missionaries, and so on. But Ephesians 4:11–13 tells us it's the role of such people to equip the saints (that is, all believers) to do the work of ministry, not to do the lion's share of it.

God does call some to vocational ministry like pastoring and overseas missions. But if you are breathing and know Jesus, you are a missionary. Where you live doesn't make you a missionary; the mission you are on (that's the *why*) does, regardless of your vocation or location.

Your Identity in Christ

It can be hard to live for Jesus in our day. I often remind young people: living for Jesus is not hard, it's impossible! That's why God gave us his Son to save us, his Spirit to live within us, his Word to guide us, and his church to encourage us. In a much more difficult time and place to live for Jesus, Peter spoke to Christians facing very real persecution. He made a powerful claim, in 1 Peter 2:9–12 (ESV):

> Where you live doesn't make you a missionary, the mission you are on does, regardless of your vocation or location.

> But you are a chosen race, a royal priesthood, a holy nation, a people for his own possession, that you may proclaim the excellencies of him who called you out of darkness into his marvelous light. Once you were not a people, but now you are God's people; once you had not received mercy, but now you have received mercy. Beloved, I urge you as sojourners and exiles to abstain from the passions of the flesh, which wage war against your soul. Keep your conduct among the Gentiles honorable, so that when they speak against you as evildoers, they may see your good deeds and glorify God on the day of visitation.

Notice again verse 9. It gives us the why I referred to earlier. Why witness? Why live for Christ? Why do what you do? You were born—or technically, re-born—to proclaim his excellence.

Not only pastors, but also someone like you. See who you are in Christ: a chosen race, a royal priesthood, a holy nation, and a people for his own possession. This is who you are. Not overweight, insecure, a poor student, incapable, or whatever you like to note as your weakness. We all have things in our lives we wish we could change and mistakes we have made, but these do not define us. Let the one who created you and who redeemed you be the one who defines you.

Then Peter tells us what we are to do: because of the why (v. 9), we can proclaim him who called us out of darkness into his marvelous light.

You were made for this. The personality you have, the limitations you have, the circumstances you face can all be a part of God making you to be a gospel-bearer uniquely designed for his glory and your good.

Then this passage gives very practical *habits*—or the how—to help you to live for Jesus and share him with others.

Negatively, abstain from the passions of the flesh. Think of it this way: pursue the things in your life that stir your affections for Jesus. Conversely, abstain from the things that tend to diminish your affections for him. Think of the things in your life that diminish your love for God, and remove them. Surround yourself with things that stir your affections for Jesus.

I need at this point to remind you of something. If you have hidden, habitual, real sin in your life you have yet to deal with, you will likely never be a passionate witness. Following Jesus means denying ourselves, taking up our cross, and following him (Luke 9:23). We can't follow Jesus with a passion when we continue to let ongoing sin reign in our lives. If this describes you, repent of your sin, forsake it, and be renewed in your faith. Perhaps talk to a spiritual mentor or pastor. You don't have to be perfect to share Jesus, but if you aren't walking with him, you won't talk about him.

Positively, Peter speaks specifically about our conduct, or how we live our lives among unbelievers. This includes both what we say and how we live. We should live honorable lives, and we should live in such a way that our good deeds bring glory to God.

Remember, we don't do good deeds to earn favor from God. Once you meet Jesus, there is nothing you can do to cause him to love you more or to love you less. Peter gives a very specific reason to do good works: it demonstrates the reality of Christianity in a practical way. There is something very attractive about a person who humbly and honorably lives life on purpose, for the good of others, to bring glory to God. This kind of life makes speaking about Jesus much more attractive as well.

> There is something very attractive about a person who humbly and honorably lives life on purpose.

Give Friendliness, Get Friendliness

After my freshman year in college I spent the summer selling books door-to-door in Virginia. It was the first time I'd been away from home on my own for a span of three months. I experienced loneliness, discouragement, and even got bitten by a dog (which has never happened to me when witnessing, by the way). There were a few bright spots, like the time I won a sales award one week for a competition in which I sold the most unusual item—a five-foot king snake I caught that week.

The summer was hard, but useful. I learned some basic people skills from the daily grind of meeting people. Talking to strangers door-to-door from morning till dark six days a week definitely helped me realize a few things about people. We have a tendency to stereotype the unknown, and we tend to make stereotypes worse than reality. When we fear something, we tend to make assumptions, which lead to stereotypes, which move toward a perspective of the worst-case scenario. I cannot count how many people I have met who, once they began to talk to people about Jesus, remarked at how open people are to talking about spiritual things.

I learned that summer that if you are friendly, most people are also friendly. I got better at my job by the practice of doing it. The more you practice witnessing, the more comfortable you will be sharing. Even more than this, as you continue to learn who you are in Christ and how God made you, you will become more comfortable sharing Christ in your own unique, uncontrived way.

Let's be clear: what we do in evangelizing is significantly different than selling a product. Yes, helpful people skills matter in both, and learning to talk and to listen to others can be learned. But here are two stunning differences between selling a product and sharing the good news. First, we are not selling something people may or may not need; we are offering a free gift that is the most vital news a person could ever know. Second, when you sell something, you are dependent on the product and on your ability to sell it. But with the gospel, we have resources not of this world.

This is why you and I can have confidence in our conversations. Our ability to talk about Jesus matters, but it has far less importance than our dependence on the gospel's power and the greatest evangelist, the Holy Spirit. Nothing activates these like believing prayer.

In 1 Thessalonians 2, Paul reminded the young believers in that church that Paul and his companions did not use coercive means, flattery, or other dubious approaches. Instead, they gave the Thessalonians not only the gospel, but also their very lives (1 Thess 2:8). Just as we are learning today that physically it's much better to eat whole foods than prepackaged fast food, sharing Christ out of who we are in a real conversation is better than a prepackaged, cookie-cutter presentation. We have nothing better to offer people than Jesus, and people need nothing more than to know our Lord.

Our Mission: To Spread the Joy of God

What if I told you that you could greatly help your verbal witness by simply changing the way you interact with those around you? What if I told you the best way to bring the gospel message of salvation in Jesus starts with our simply bringing joy to our world?

Our hesitancy to witness can come from the way we view our world. Perhaps you have the view that everything in our world is wretched, evil, and out to destroy every good and godly thing we hold dear. Satan is certainly real, and we do wrestle with the world, the flesh, and the devil. Our world is fallen, but our enemy is neither the unsaved people we meet nor the society in which we live. Our war is with powers, principalities, and evil beyond this world (Eph 6). People are not our enemy; people are blinded by our enemy. Forster explains how we should bring the joy of God to those around us:

> The joy of God equips us with knowledge, freedom, and strength. . . . Our identities and motivations are invested in loving others rather than serving ourselves. And we have the power of the Spirit to help us carry that love through in action. Shame on us if we're not experts in making the world a better place! This—and nothing else—is what can create a real encounter with the holistic joy of God for people outside the church. If they encounter Christianity through our efforts to leverage secondary assets (politics, scholarship, worldview, evangelism, emotions, causes), they will not encounter the joy of God. *But when they see that the total Christian life makes a radical difference in homes, work-places, and communities, they will want to know why. Then they will know that the joy of God is a real thing. Then they will know that there is a real supernatural power working in the lives of Christians.*[30]

Forster testifies to what that looks like when he describes a relative who walked away from the faith when young. Some fifty years later she asked Greg if he and his wife would go with her to see the movie *The Passion of the Christ*. After the movie the couple talked with her about Christ. She reflected on all the people she knew who were believers who exhibited joy in their lives and the impact that made. That day, she trusted Christ as Savior, but it was the impact of the lives of those she knew and the joy they demonstrated that evidenced the reality of the gospel.

Recently my friend Jason Gaston, a pastor at Summit Church in Raleigh-Durham, spoke in a class. He quoted a statement used a lot at Summit: "Do what you do well for the glory of God strategically for the mission of God." Imagine if each of us lived that way daily. Today, do what you do well. Be the person God made you to be. Use that for God's mission, first by bringing joy to your world, and then by speaking openly about your Savior.

> Do what you do well for the glory of God strategically for the mission of God.
> —Summit Church

{ CHAPTER 5 }

Ignition and Transition: Conversation Starters and Signposts

Philip . . . heard him reading the prophet Isaiah, and said, "Do you understand what you're reading?" "How can I," he said, "unless someone guides me?" So he invited Philip to come up and sit with him.

—Acts 8:30–31

I just had coffee with a young man, Ronnie,[31] who I led to Christ a few years ago, in the very coffee shop where I met him. We first met when he served my table at a local restaurant I frequented.

"Remember how you kept coming into the restaurant after the first time I served you?" he recalled. Over the years I've asked hundreds of servers how I might pray for them as I said grace before the meal. That day, a connection started from that simple request onward (he asked me to pray for a family member). Soon he visited our church, and in a few weeks I led him to Christ. He moved away soon after, but he always connects with me when he comes to town, and we always talk about his spiritual growth.

I've seen a few folks come to faith by simply asking to pray for them before a meal in a restaurant where they served me. I always leave a good tip, by the way!

What if I told you that starting a conversation about Jesus or turning a conversation toward the gospel is simpler than you think?

Avoid the Paralysis of Analysis: Overthinking Conversations

I hear it all the time. The hardest thing about sharing Jesus once you know the gospel is transitioning a conversation to talk specifically about Jesus. I promise, it's not as hard as you think.

Principle 5: Effective evangelistic conversations connect the unchanging gospel with the specific issues people face.

Picture a person you personally know who doesn't know Jesus. Let's call him Jerome. Here's a simple, effective way to speak to Jerome used by my accountability partner and men's pastor at the Creek (our church), Jim Gillespie:

Jim: "Nice to meet you, Jerome. I'm a pastor at Richland Creek Community Church, and we believe God loves us, but we are in a mess, and only Jesus can fix that mess. He changed me and he can change you."

Jim simply introduces the gospel briefly as a part of describing who he is. It's natural and effective for him.

Okay, so you are not a pastor (or a biker) like Jim. That may be a bit direct for you. Try this: "Jerome, I've been a follower of Jesus for a long time. I really want to learn to tell others about how Jesus changed my life. Could I share my story with you, and then could you tell me if what I'm saying makes sense to you?"

How are those for examples of a remarkable, hip, and cool approach? Nah, they are none of those. But they are honest.

We need to focus less on speaking cleverly and more on sharing honestly. The early believers couldn't help but speak about Jesus (Acts 4:20). That's honesty.

If we honestly love Jesus and people we can honestly and confidently talk to them.

A year ago I had a student tell me of a conversation he had with a neighbor. As the conversation moved along he felt strongly he should speak to the neighbor about Jesus. But the conversation ended with no mention of the Savior. I assured him he was the sorriest Christian on earth and a failure for not speaking up about Jesus. No, I didn't say that!

I challenged him: whenever he thought about speaking to someone about Jesus, just start talking about Jesus in the conversation the moment the thought comes to mind. Then, watch to see what happens. About two months later our class rejoiced with him as that very neighbor had come to Jesus, because my student started talking instead of just thinking about it.

His problem: overthinking. The paralysis of analysis. Read the Scriptures and note that whenever the Lord said to someone to arise and go somewhere, almost always they just got up and went. We need to obey more quickly and obsess less frequently.

I want to give you some practical encouragement about starting conversations and transitioning. But here is the deal: at some point, you still have to do it. And you can. If you want to become healthier, you can't just think about getting in shape. You have to get moving.

Think of a challenge you faced in your life, big or small, whether one you chose (like running a 10K) or one thrust upon you (like a health issue). While challenges are, well, challenging, there is something life-giving about facing a challenge and surpassing it.

The question is, why is sharing Jesus so hard for us?

Time for a Revolution in Evangelism

To see where we are going we need to first look back, so let me channel my inner history nerd to give a very simple overview of church life in recent history. Over a century ago the Industrial Revolution led to *mass production* as large factories drew people to cities.[32] Henry Ford and others after him perfected the assembly line and the capacity to make large numbers of products en masse. This reality and the rapid urbanization of the times matched perfectly with the most effective tool of evangelism in the latter nineteenth and early twentieth centuries: the urban mass meeting. D. L. Moody pioneered this approach that others then followed. While Ford mass-produced his automobiles, the church witnessed mass conversions in these meetings.

As factories grew and urbanization increased, more and more people worked with others in increasingly impersonal workplaces, developing the forty-hour work week, which in turn created a growing yearning for the weekend and less appreciation for the job. For too many, one's job became a necessary means to a greater end (the weekend, vacation, leisure) and less a place we valued. "Punch your time card, do your job, and live for the weekend" became a reality for millions. No wonder so many today have the "3 S's" mind-set toward church: As long as I *show up* on Sundays, *serve* in some way (take up the offering, sing in the choir, and so on), and am a *steward* (give a little money), I'm doing just fine as a Christian.

Millions of American Christians have no idea that this is practically how they live out their faith. Show up, check in, consume some religious goods, and then live your life as you like.

In the middle of the twentieth century, things changed somewhat. Mass production continued, but we also saw the rise of mass media. The television escalated this shift, making advertisers grow in influence. "Try this product"; "Use this brand," we were told. It was the day of the Fuller Brush salesman going door-to-door with his prepackaged sales pitch. At this time, we saw the rise of programmatic approaches to ministry in the church, including packaged evangelism training. The Church Growth Movement arose as well, offering specialists to help diagnose issues in a particular church setting and offer processes for change. This proved to be as effective in this era for a time as mass crusades had been previously.

Don't read this and hear me saying these specific methods are all bad, for they aren't; they have in fact helped millions turn to Christ and countless believers to grow. They fit well with the times in the past and can still reach people today. But they had the unintended consequence of showing believers that the way to grow as a disciple of Jesus is not by your own ability through the Spirit's work to self-feed and grow daily, but by attending as many programs at the church building as possible. This has also created a lowest-common-denominator, one-size-fits-all approach to discipleship that has condemned entire generations to unintended spiritual mediocrity.

But times changed again, and they can change in the church as well. We have moved from a mass production age to a mass media era to the information age. The Internet has changed everything. This has led to our time currently, in which ideas rule the day, and especially ideas that are spread through stories. Look at television today and see the infomercials using testimonies and note the reality shows in which your neighbor could be a star.

Add to that the sudden ascension of social media as the dominant force on the Internet. Everyone has an idea today, it seems. Individuals can have great influence, whether it's a Mark Zuckerberg inventing Facebook, or the founders of Craigslist or Wikipedia, or lesser-known people who sell their wares on Etsy. We live in a time when the individual has been given again the opportunity to let their ideas flourish.

What an amazing opportunity for believers to recover the biblical reality that you have been given in Christ all you need for life and godliness. You were made in the image of God uniquely to bring glory to him unlike anyone else. Don't be mistaken; the church is still vitally involved in this process, keeping us from either doctrinal error or rampant individualism. But the church must do a better job of helping each believer have the tools to grow spiritually, to study the Word, and to share your faith without being dependent on a prepackaged program or a gifted evangelist.

You can, by the power of the Spirit, through the wisdom from the Word, with a life bathed in prayer and connected to the local church, be a self-feeder who becomes not a clone of other believers, but one who, uniquely made in the image of God, can reflect Christ as God created you to be and to do.

The Source of the Story Is the Source of Your Strength

How do you know the Holy Spirit is leading you? How can you tell you are walking daily, moment by moment, in step with Jesus? The same gospel story that changed you also gives you the capacity to move beyond your fears and insecurities to talk about Jesus. Before you can ignite a conversation, God needs to light a fire in you.

> The Father sees us, the Spirit guides us, and the Son of God compels us.

Let me encourage you to remember that nothing you or I do for God is done alone. The Father sees us, the Spirit guides us, and the Son of God compels us. Here are resources you have to help you as you reach out to others.

Expand Your Resources: The Power of Prayer[33]

Linking Prayer and Evangelism

You can't evangelize effectively on a consistent basis without prayer. Witnessing is spiritual warfare. How can prayer help us?

Pray for boldness to witness (see Acts 4:24–31). I mentioned a simple prayer at the beginning of this book: "God, give me an opportunity to speak to someone about Jesus, give me wisdom to see it, and give me boldness to take it." If you've been praying that daily, I'm confident you've seen its effect. If not, start today.

Pray in the Spirit's power. In Ephesians 6, Paul followed his discussion of the armor of God with a request for believers to pray for bold proclamation of the gospel (Eph 6:18–20). Prayer is seen as an indispensable part of the armor of God, as is the Word, the sword of the Spirit. Paul exhorted the Ephesians to pray for "utterance," or *parrhesia,* which means an openness to share the gospel. This is the expression translated "boldness" in Acts 4:29, 31. Paul was in prison as he wrote these words, asking for courage to share Christ.

J. D. Greear has a great saying about the Holy Spirit from the subtitle of his book *Jesus, Continued.* "The Spirit inside you," he notes, "is better than Jesus beside you."[34] It's his way of pointing out what we so often overlook, the power of the Spirit in every believer. The Spirit is not for super saints or the unusually gifted; he dwells in every Christian. If you are saved, you have the Spirit. You have all the Spirit you will ever have or need. Ephesians 1:13–14 tells us the Spirit sealed us as God's children the moment we believed. As we live daily, bearing the fruit of the Spirit (see Gal 5:22–23) in front of others, we become the aroma of Christ to those we encounter (see 2 Cor 2:15 ESV).

Pray for harvesters to join you. In Matthew 9:38, Jesus, seeing the multitude wandering about like sheep with no shepherd, encouraged prayer for the Lord of the harvest to send laborers. We should pray that God would awaken believers to the need of the world for the gospel. We must pray for God to call out those who would go to the ends of the earth proclaiming Christ. How would your neighborhood or workplace look if all believers there sought to have gospel conversations regularly with others?

Pray for those who need Jesus. Here are five ways you can pray for those who need Christ:

1. Ask God to open their spiritual eyes (2 Cor 4:4).
2. Ask God to give them ears to hear (Matt 13:15), faith to believe (Acts 20:21), and a will to respond (Rom 10:9).
3. Ask God to send people into their lives to witness to them (Matt 9:38).
4. Ask God for ways to build caring relationships (1 Cor 9:22).
5. Ask God for an opportunity to invite them to an event where the gospel is shared (Luke 14:23).

Spiritual work like witnessing needs spiritual power. God uses both the spiritual resources he's made available to you through a new birth and the talents, gifts, and passions he formed in you. For some people the biggest hurdle to effective witnessing is practical. You simply need some practical ways to have conversations with others.

Becoming a Conversationalist in a Social Media World: Five Approaches

The next time you find yourself in a public place, notice how many people are having conversations without a phone visible versus those employing their phones. Also track the presence of earbuds. We've lost the ability to have meaningful conversations today in a sea of smartphones. Psychologist Sherry Turkle wrote *Alone Together,* which describes in painful detail the impact of texting, email, and social media on our ability to have honest conversations with people. "In today's workplace," she writes in the *New York Times,* "young people who have grown up fearing conversation show up on the job wearing earphones. . . . [W]e are together, but each of us is in our own bubble, furiously connected to keyboards and tiny touch screens." She observes the cocooning effect of our smartphone world: "Texting and e-mail and posting let us present the self we want to be. This means we can edit. And if we wish to, we can delete. Or retouch: the voice, the flesh, the face, the body. Not too much, not too little—just right."[35]

In other words, we have learned to be around people without exposing our real selves, fabricating a profile that matches what we want people to see on Facebook or Twitter instead of the real flesh-and-bones people we are.

I'm writing a book on having conversations with people about Jesus in a day when we are pretty lame at having conversations. What an incredible opportunity we have! Underneath the veneer of social media, we all really want to have deep conversations, intimate relationships, and authentic lives.

The very world technology has created, which is great for connecting but also lousy at real community, may be the very open door for humble, honest, life-giving conversations about Jesus. I'm finding a lot of young adults are starving for real community and genuine conversations.

It's vital to develop personal conversational skills that fit who you are. Here are five practical ways to engage people in conversation.[36]

Approach One: The Power of Story and Stories (Everyone Has a Story)

One of the simplest and most helpful ways to move a conversation to the gospel is to simply ask someone to tell you his or her story. Everyone has a story, right? In fact, each person's life represents a metanarrative, even as in the Bible. I could ask you about your musical interests and we could talk for a while. That's your musical story. We could talk sports, family, work, and so on. All these individual storylines of a person's life help to tell their whole story. It's pretty natural for me to talk to a guy about his story and then show how God's great story intersects with ours. If you want to talk about Jesus to a friend or family member whose story you already know, you could ask about a specific aspect of their story, from movie interests to entertainment choices, from favorite foods to favorite places.

When I meet someone at a coffee shop and ask about his story, I'm not just fishing for a "hook" to witness; I really enjoy getting to know people. But as an ambassador commissioned by Jesus and filled with love both for my Lord and my friend, I naturally want to connect the two.

Invariably, I tell some part of my story of meeting Christ, my testimony of salvation. Your story is amazing. You don't have to be a former drug addict or a gangster to have a powerful testimony: the Christ of your experience matters far more than the particulars of your experience with Christ. If you've never shared your story of coming to Christ with someone, start there. Perhaps you've never written out your own story of salvation. You can do so following this simple outline:

- What was your life like before meeting Jesus?
- How did Jesus change your life? (Include both an explanation of the gospel and the circumstances when you trusted him.)
- How is your life changing from when you met him until now?

You can hear the other person's story, then share your story of conversion, followed by asking, "Has anything like this ever happened to you?"

Approach Two: Ask Good Questions

Asking thoughtful questions can help transition a conversation to the gospel. Let's say you have a friend you want to talk to about Jesus, but you can't seem to get over the hill of moving a conversation in that direction. Asking questions helps. I'm not talking about questions where we're not really interested in the answer, but just want to get the person to hear us. You know, like when we ask someone how he is doing and we don't even pay attention to what he says (I'm guilty at times).

I'm talking about questions that open up a person to talk about things that matter. A student of mine named Joshua emailed me, describing how some questions I wrote in another place helped him:

> I am a student who took your evangelism class. During the class I read your *Evangelism Handbook* and three questions from the book help me immensely in sharing the good news of Jesus Christ. Those questions are:
>
> - What is your faith background?
> - When you attend church, where do you go?
> - In your opinion, what is a real Christian?
>
> I have approached people who were both strangers and those who I have worked with for years and just asked those questions. . . . Every time I've used these questions it has opened up conversation to share Christ. In fact, these questions have helped in alleviating a struggle I have always found with sharing Christ, which is having a way to bridge to the gospel.

Josh went on to tell me two examples of people he had led to Christ, one a stranger and one a coworker, starting with these questions. Whether he knew the person well or had just met him, he found it not difficult at all to share his love for Jesus and the person's need to repent and believe by first asking questions. It may be that simple, honest questions like these are all you need.

In Acts 8, with Philip and the Ethiopian eunuch, we see the value of asking a good question. Philip was led by God to join the eunuch in his chariot. He heard the eunuch reading from Isaiah. "Do you understand what you are reading?" he asked. You can ask pretty much anyone who is reading anything what he is reading and why, and move into a conversation that allows you to tell why reading the Bible matters to you. The eunuch replied that he needed someone to guide him. Talk about a divine appointment! Philip did just that, and led him to Christ. The more we seek to have conversations about God, the more God-appointments we will have.

The grand narrative of Scripture helps us with asking key worldview questions answered by the gospel:

- How did everything begin? (Creation)
- What went wrong? (Fall)
- What can be done? (Rescue)
- What does the future hold? (Restoration)

Asking questions helps us get to know the other person so we can speak to her more specifically about Jesus.

Approach Three: Genuine Affirmation and Encouragement

All of us at some point think about God and our relationship to him. When people you know do so, you want them to think about you. Being an encouraging and affirming person helps to open those opportunities. We've created an "us against them" mentality toward the lost that can hinder us from affirming anything we see in them. You don't have to embrace another person's lifestyle to affirm or encourage them. You don't have to agree with someone's life choices to affirm him as someone made in the image of God.

> You can affirm someone personally without endorsing their lifestyle completely.

Anya,[37] a Muslim student originally from Africa, came to faith when I taught at a university years ago. I hadn't personally developed a tried and true way to witness to Muslims, but I did believe the gospel had the power to save people from whatever perspective they had. She worked on campus, which allowed me to see her regularly. I always sought to encourage her. There was a time when I had the opportunity to speak to her about Jesus; at that point she believed Jesus to be a prophet, but not the Son of God.

After taking my class, Anya wrote me a note: "I now know Jesus is not only a prophet—he is God! He has changed me, and I have never been so happy!" The most significant impact I made on Anya beyond the sheer power of the gospel was this: I encouraged her and affirmed her. Not only did I speak to her about Christ, but I also regularly thanked her for being such a good worker on campus, and for her generally friendly demeanor. I sought to treat her as a person, not a project. You can affirm the image of God in people who don't walk with him. We do this all the time in our acknowledgment of talented actors or athletes; they may not be Christians, but we can see God has gifted them with talent.

I once saw a bisexual youth come to Christ where I preached. I was told her background and made it a point to get to know her in meal times and other informal gatherings over the weekend. I observed her unique hairstyle, telling her our daughter Hannah is a stylist and I'm fascinated by the diversity of styles and colors people who have hair (unlike me, since I'm totally bald) wear. We talked about art and music. I talked a lot about my relationship with Hannah. Before the weekend was over she trusted Christ. Because I chose to affirm her as a person without condoning her lifestyle (she knew where I stood on that), she listened to the message I shared. When we treat people with respect and show genuine interest in them, we can speak the gospel clearly and plainly to them. Turns out she was really hungry for the gospel, but hid behind the security of her lifestyle choice as a façade to cover a lot of pain.

Approach Four: Speak to the Person's Mind and Heart

What if I told you the key to reaching most people has less to do with the way you deal with them intellectually and more to do with the way you touch them emotionally? Much research has been done on this in recent years: on connecting with people via emotional intelligence, for instance. I could bore you with talk about the limbic system of the brain, where the emotions lie, but let me simply make this point: we were made to know God, and we were made to be in community with one another. This goes beyond our intellectual affirmations alone.

That's why evangelistic conversations with someone can feel more like a counseling encounter, seeking to apply the gospel to the struggles of life, and less like a debate, where I'm trying to give intellectual truths alone.

> Sometimes evangelistic conversations can feel more like a counseling encounter and less like a debate.

Scripture doesn't affirm the homosexual lifestyle, but our society today largely does. A significant reason our country has shifted dramatically toward affirming gay marriage is because those leading the gay rights movement focused more on winning hearts before winning minds. Tying the gay rights movement to the civil rights movement created an emotional connection. That the gay rights movement has more in common with the movement of the sexual revolution in the 1960s than the civil rights movement has been almost totally lost, and the conversation has focused less on the physical, sexual activity at the heart of homosexuality and more on the emotional: if we love each other, that's all that matters.

Communicating the gospel is as much an art as a science. The science is in the truth: the unchanging, life-giving, eternally significant good news about Jesus. The art comes in taking who you are (the person God made you to be) and connecting with who the other person is, in a way that does more than offer information, as valuable as that is.

People tend to fall into three categories in terms of how they relate to the world, process information, and develop relationships. Some are primarily thinkers, or people who deal with reality first intellectually. They give a great focus to *orthodoxy*, or sound thinking. If this is you, you love subjects like apologetics and theology. You may be one who enjoys a good debate. You also may become impatient with other believers who don't share your love for defending the faith or studying theology. But not everyone is wired like you.

Others tend to be doers, people who want to put their faith into action. I'm wired this way. We want to do something that matters, to find a cause we can impact. The word for this is *orthopraxy*, or right actions.

The third group are people who really care for others, who tend to wear their hearts on their sleeves, those who love God (or whatever they call their spirituality) deeply and care for people passionately. The word for this is *orthopathy*, or right affections.

Which of these is correct? All of the above.[38] Each of us should value all these: truth matters, truth that works matters, and truth that moves us to love God and others matters. But if you're like my students, you can see that one of these best describes you. In fact, there are entire traditions that tend toward one or another. Reformed and Bible churches tend to be marked more by the trait of orthodoxy; my own Southern Baptist world, driven to global evangelism, is activist or orthopraxic in focus; more contemplative groups and those more emotive in worship, such as many in the Charismatic tradition, would be described as leaning toward orthopathy.

This can have a significant impact on our conversations with people about Jesus. This is truer the more we know someone; if I have a lost friend who is an activist, I'm more naturally going to focus on how Christianity cares for causes like social justice issues. If I'm talking with someone who is more intellectually wired I'm going to introduce bigger issues of coherence and truth. If I have a friend who is very passionate about people and cares about the disenfranchised, I will seek to show him how Christ identified with the weak and calls us in the Bible to care for the widow, the orphan, the stranger, and the poor.

Approach Five: Connect beneath the Surface

What we want to do in sharing Christ is to get beneath the surface of where we live to the real issues people face. This is where relating to someone based on their passion or pain (see chapter 3) helps.

This often means you have to get to know someone well before they will open up. But don't assume this is always the case. I've seen strangers, from servers in restaurants to passengers on airplanes, opening up their whole lives in the first conversation I had with them, because they could tell (as noted before) I cared about them, I believed what I was sharing, and I showed a genuine relationship with God to them.

The best way to learn the approach that most fits you is to put it into practice. I often incorporate some aspect of each of these in a conversation; you too can develop a way to talk about Christ that is biblical, practical, and personal.

CHAPTER 6

Let Them Help You: Start with Them and They Will Point to the Gospel

A woman of Samaria came to draw water. "Give me a drink," Jesus said to her, because his disciples had gone into town to buy food. "How is it that you, a Jew, ask for a drink from me, a Samaritan woman?" she asked him. For Jews do not associate with Samaritans. Jesus answered, "If you knew the gift of God, and who is saying to you, 'Give me a drink,' you would ask him, and he would give you living water."

—John 4:7–10

I once spent a Friday night watching a remarkable personal witness. I watched Darrell talk to person after person, calmly, graciously, and intentionally. We had the joy of seeing one come to faith that night, which was awesome. But what stayed with me more than anything was not how he shared

Christ, or even how he initiated conversations, although I learned there as well.

What struck me was his attitude toward people. I don't mean in this instance the fact that he was sweet to people, although he was. Relationships obviously mattered to him. Even going out and knocking on doors to talk to total strangers, he sought to make friends, not visits. Here is the lesson I learned: *he truly expected people to be open to hear about Christ.* He assumed they would be friendly. His aim was not to close a deal or drop some truth, but to meet a new friend. His calm, kind demeanor helped, but his genuine expectation that every person he met truly had a longing to know God, whether that person realized it or not, caused conversations to open up about Christ. There is potency in expectancy when we talk about Jesus.

Principle 6: Expect people to be open to the gospel, and learn to share Jesus where they live.

Our goal in conversations can never be to communicate the gospel impersonally, but to share the truth of Jesus personally. Learning to see an individual as someone for whom Christ died and as a potential friend rather than as a notch on a gospel gun belt opens the way for conversations. As I've taught my students to think of evangelism as making friends instead of contacts, it's been a game changer for many.

Relieving the Pressure

One of the reasons we freeze up when talking about Jesus is the unnecessary pressure we put on ourselves, like thinking we are the other person's only hope, confusing ourselves with Jesus, or feeling we have to have the perfect "hook" to pull the gospel into the conversation. I felt the pressure to perform for years myself. I was the evangelism director for the State Convention of Baptists in Indiana at age thirty-one. I starting teaching evangelism to ministry students in my early thirties, and by my mid-thirties I found myself teaching evangelism at an extremely evangelistically focused, growing seminary. There were days I felt enormous pressure to witness.

I thought that came with the territory. It actually came from my failure to understand my identity in Jesus. Here is the cool part: when I really began to understand that my "job performance" as an evangelism professor, and, more important, my walk with Jesus, was not tied directly to the number of people I won to Christ (or even how often I witnessed), I began to experience a wonderful release of pressure. But here is the amazingly awesome thing: This realization did not cause me to witness less. It caused me to listen more when I did witness.

You won't lose your salvation if you don't witness; you also won't lose weight if you eat junk food relentlessly and never exercise. But just as eating well and exercise will

> Share out of the joy of knowing Jesus, not out of fear of failing him.

make you enjoy life more (and probably for longer), sharing Jesus will bring so much joy to your life and glory to God. Share out of the joy of knowing Jesus, not out of fear of failing him.

Initiate a Gospel Conversation in a Variety of Spheres

Jesus did this. He naturally transitioned conversations to talk about spiritual things. Reading the Gospels to learn from Jesus' interaction with people will help your witness. Think of the Samaritan woman in John 4. Jesus had to go to Samaria to reach those most would not touch. I want to be like that Jesus, don't you?

When Jesus met the woman at the well, he was weary—exhausted, in fact. His disciples scurried away to find food. This anonymous, immoral Samaritan lady showed up to get water, and there sat a thirsty Jewish guy. Then, he did the unthinkable: he asked her for a drink (v. 7).

He was thirsty, after all. But Jesus broke some taboos you can see in verse 9: the woman couldn't believe a Jewish man would ask her for a drink. Jesus did something more, as he used the analogy of water to explain to her the source of eternal life. I won't recount the whole conversation, but I want you to see how Jesus took an everyday occurrence, the need for water we can all understand, and gave it a spiritual focus. He started in her world and showed her his kingdom. I want to help you refocus conversations like this.

It's easier to learn a scripted presentation to say the same thing to people every time, but learning to share Christ even as you apply the gospel to your life will be more profitable to your own spiritual development. It also helps us not to be awkward around others. Some Christians have theological B.O.: they believe correctly, but stink about it when talking. You can learn to share Jesus naturally in a variety of spheres. By "spheres" I mean all the avenues of life we experience in culture. This certainly includes church, but also involves everything from our kids' education to politics, from sports interests to vocational choices. It includes the world where your kids play in a rec league, local events in your town, and even the lawn company that cares for your yard.

My colleague Bruce Ashford wrote a helpful book called *Every Square Inch* to help believers relate their faith to culture today. Bruce observes the vital role of both showing and sharing Christ in the world:

> Our jobs are opportunities to witness about Christ precisely by backing up our words with actions. Not only do we let people know verbally that Christ is Lord, but we also do our work in a way that is shaped by Christ and his Word. This combination of word and deed can be powerful. For many people, the workplace is their best opportunity to meet unbelievers who might have

never heard the gospel or seen a Christian living out the gospel in front of their very eyes.[39]

Bruce notes the four areas in which we are called to live out our faith: our home, church, workplace, and community. Too many of us focus on the first two and ignore the other two. From this he suggests several spheres in which we can engage others with biblical truth. I make no claim to be an expert in all these fields. What I want to do is suggest a couple of ideas in specific spheres to illustrate how you might engage someone in conversation. If you live and work in one of these spheres you would likely be far more capable than I at developing ways to integrate the gospel story with a given sphere.

Doing so may prove to be one of the most helpful ways for you to grow as a Christian and to make your faith come alive in the everyday world. Here are only a few examples.

The Arts

At age fifteen our son Josh was already an accomplished drummer. One day he sat at the computer watching a DVD of Carter Beauford, the remarkable drummer of the Dave Matthews Band.

"Dad," Josh said, "why is it most of the best musicians are not Christians?"

Fair question. I mumbled some answer about Christianity being more about the message, so lyrics mattered more than musical ability. Then I stopped.

"Son," I told him, "it's basically because in our day the church has largely given up the arts to the world."

We've created one of the most elaborate Christian subcultures in history, and one of the negative effects has been the development of "Christian art," which often means ripping something from the world, sticking a cross on it, and calling it art. Compare that to C. S. Lewis. Ashford observes:

Lewis wanted to translate Christianity into popular language for ordinary people who were not theologians. In his fiction texts, he tried to create in his readers a longing for God, and to help them "see" the gospel in concrete form. He called this type of writing *praeparatione evangelica*, or "preparation for the gospel." So for Lewis, "evangelism" is something that Christians do with their whole lives, not only through interpersonal encounters, but in the work they undertake and the shape of their professional lives.[40]

I'm praying for a new day in the church where the arts again play a vital role in our gospel work. I've found that allowing a person interested in the arts to share her passion for her craft can lead to a conversation in which the gospel storyline can intersect with her interest in the arts. Showing we respect and appreciate a person's interest in the arts will often open a door to a gospel conversation, whether we know about the specific art under discussion. Having an appetite for learning and for getting to know people helps a lot here.

Here's a simple, practical way you can talk with someone who paints, for instance. You can talk about primary colors, and the way you can take red, yellow, and blue to make the amazing diversity of colors we see all around us daily. You can take any visual art form and reduce it ultimately to these colors. Life is like that, isn't it? As complicated as our lives are, we can boil life down to a few, basic, ultimate questions. You can reduce almost any storyline in literature to a handful of specific plotlines. You can dissolve the many chemicals in our body to a few essential elements. There are a few fundamental questions people ask:

Where did everything come from?

What has gone wrong in the world?

What can be done about this?

What does the future hold?

These are primary questions of life, just like there are primary colors to all we see.

Business

Have you ever met someone who wanted to start a business so they could declare total failure and file for bankruptcy? Not likely. We start a business to succeed, not to fail. Businesses also follow certain unchanging principles of commerce, and follow business ethics. Sure, some don't, but over the long haul the overwhelming number of businesses that prosper follow both sound economic principles and some code of ethics.

In his book *Good to Great,* Jim Collins analyzes major corporations that experienced a lengthy season of decline followed by years of quality growth. He studied the leaders of those businesses to find out common characteristics. Guess what the two most defining marks of "level 5" leaders were? The same two marks that were used to describe Moses and Paul, and the same two marks that epitomized the life of Jesus. Humility and intense devotion to their company marked these CEOs.[41]

Why do I tell you this? I'm no businessman; I'm a teacher and gospel minister. But I've worked with a lot of businessmen and have never had a problem relating to them with information like that which I just gave you. You can talk about the desire for businesses to prosper and relate that to the image of God in every person, which makes in us a desire for our lives to matter. You can talk about business ethics and explain how we all see the need for boundaries of behavior, and we see this clearly in the way God set up the world.

> No matter your vocation or your location, if you know Jesus and you are breathing, you are a missionary.

This also affects how you think about work as a believer. Whether you are a butcher, baker, or candlestick maker, or a doctor, lawyer, preacher, or teacher, you can live on mission for Jesus. No matter your vocation or your location, if you know Jesus and you are breathing, you are a missionary. Thinking of ways to have conversations with those in your sphere of vocation is vital for your witness.

Sports

We are a people too often obsessed with sports (Roll Tide!). No one has ever cheered for a team to go winless, right? No, we want our teams to win. And we don't like it when our team loses because the other team cheated. We have a sense of right and wrong and a sense of victory even with something as trivial as sports. Why?

I see this in the related world of health and fitness. I listen to a lot of fitness podcasts. I've noticed a consistent pattern with fitness pros. No one talks about mediocrity. They all push people to excellence. Sport does that; it pushes us to win, not lose.

These experts continually emphasize three things: First, every person is unique, so there is no one-size-fits-all diet or fitness fix. A low-carb diet might pave the way to health for one fellow, but it may train-wreck another dude's physical chemistry. There is no one-size-fits-all way to witness; it's the same with fitness. Sounds a lot like the *imago Dei*, doesn't it? God created every person uniquely for his glory, whether we realize it or not.

> There is something remarkably attractive about someone who lives a disciplined, humble life with purpose.

Second, leaders I listen to repeatedly talk about the value of community. God made us communal. That's why the church is more than a religious institution; it's family. Finally, they continually note in some way or another the importance of spirituality as it relates to your physical life. Most of these folks are not Christians, mind you. But they see the importance of spirituality, of meditation, or prayer, to one's physical well-being.

You can add to your witness before saying a word by showing how you value your physical body as well as your spiritual health. There is something remarkably attractive about someone who lives a disciplined, humble life with purpose. Most people who talk about fitness talk about motivation. You or I can easily talk about our motivation:

- Our bodies are temples of the Holy Spirit (1 Cor 6:20), so we want to give God glory by taking care of ourselves.
- Bodily discipline is of some merit to God (1 Tim 4:8), but of even greater importance is our spiritual growth. Our desire to be healthy physically should be surpassed by our desire to be growing spiritually.
- We see life as only a brief opportunity to serve the Lord before worshiping him forever, so we take care of our bodies so we can serve him as long as we can as effectively as possible.

We could talk about other realms, like education, science, and politics. In all these realms we can find features that take us back to our desire for something more, or for justice, or for something that gives us hope. All these themes can take us to a conversation about Jesus, the Justifier, the only true hope for the world.

Others Can Initiate a Gospel Conversation for You

Most of the times we read of Jesus speaking to individuals involve people coming to him: In Matthew 9, for instance, a group brought a paralytic to him. Later, John's disciples approached him, followed by a leader concerned about his daughter. Nicodemus sought Jesus at night (I call that "Nic at Night") in John 3. If we walk with Jesus and seek to bring the joy of God to others around us and to our community, some will approach us as well. When they do, it would be weird not to talk about Jesus.

Many times others initiate a conversation not directly aimed at spiritual things, but we, like Jesus at the well with the Samaritan woman, can turn the conversation to spiritual things. The spheres noted above offer only a sampling of the many ways you can naturally turn a conversation to the gospel, not to drop a sales pitch, but to share the passion of your life, the good news!

Remember this is the beginning of a journey, so give yourself time to learn how to speak to others of Jesus out of who you are. Don't settle for the "show up at church, give some money, and serve at the building" approach to Christianity that has left so many unchallenged and apathetic. Push yourself to grow and learn; you were born for this. The mind-set to have is this: instead of figuring out a way to force the gospel into the conversation, listen to people to hear ways redemption would relate to them. Because evangelism is caught more than taught, find a more experienced witness and go with him to observe and learn. We can all learn from others ways to grow in our witness.

My friend Jonathan Dodson has a wonderful, conversational way of doing this.[42] I've taught this to some believers at my church, and they've found it to be extremely helpful. He developed his personal approach from the arena of counseling. The approach can be summarized as listen, empathize, and redemptively retell a person's story:

- *Listen* **to their story.** Simply ask them to tell you their story, where they are from, family life, and so on. If you already know them, ask them about specific aspects of their story, such as how long they lived where they are, how they got there, what makes them stay, and so on.
- *Empathize* **with their story.** When people find that you're interested in their story and can perceive you really care, they often open up and tell a lot of things,

some of which may make you blush. Don't judge. Don't react. Don't freak out. Sometimes we try too hard to be the Bible Answer Man or Woman when we really just need to listen. Instead of immediately trying to fix the person's life, empathize. I asked a young man to tell me his story recently. He has been through a lot of pain, and has had people mistreat him. Instead of telling him to suck it up and be a man or launching into a philosophical speech on theodicy (the problem of evil), I listened, and then shared with him my own pain, like how getting an artificial hip at age thirty-eight was not only physically painful, but it was emotionally painful when I realized I could no longer wrestle with my kids or do other things I so enjoyed.

- *Retell* **their story redemptively.** Give them a vision for what life might look like if Jesus entered their story. Speak of God's creative work, and how we are all uniquely made individuals, uniquely made by God to know him. Share about the wretchedness of sin and how we are all broken because of that. But offer to them how Jesus' work on the cross has healed your own brokenness, and is helping with struggles you now face. Be real, and be honest. Share your struggles. Above all, exalt Jesus.

CHAPTER 7

Talk, but with More than Words

In your hearts honor Christ the Lord as holy, always being pre-
pared to make a defense to anyone who asks you for a reason for
the hope that is in you; yet do it with gentleness and respect, hav-
ing a good conscience, so that, when you are slandered, those who
revile your good behavior in Christ may be put to shame.

—1 Peter 3:15–16 ESV

Who do you know who needs to know Jesus?
It's hard to have conversations with lost people when we don't know any, right? You probably know more than you realize. Let's take a look at your current relationships.

Many years ago I read a book called *Concentric Circles of Concern* by W. Oscar Thompson Jr.[43] A chart in the book helps us to see those around us with gospel eyes. Grab a pen and paper and take a look at the chart below. Take a few minutes to write down the names of people in each circle. Start at the most inward circle just outside yourself.

Do you have close *family* members who need to know Jesus? Other *relatives* you see on occasion?

What about *friends*? Jesus was criticized for being a friend of sinners (not a friend of sin!). Do you have friends who are more than evangelism projects, who are real friends who need Jesus? I have a fishing buddy who to this point has not come to Christ. I love this friend. I hope he meets Jesus.

How about your *neighbors*? Do you actually know your neighbors? When speaking, I often ask people in the audience to raise their hand if they grew up in a Christian home. It's usually around 80 to 90 percent. I then ask those people to raise their hand if their families ever talked about reaching their unsaved neighbors.

It's usually no more than 10 percent.

We Christian families raise our children as if we were atheists in our neighborhoods. Our neighbors who don't know Jesus are a heartbeat away from eternity without God! I'm not trying to shame you but to get you to think.

Every Christmas Michelle makes a nice, personal Christmas gift for each of our neighbors. She's great with crafts, and we have neighbors who tell us the most precious gift they've received at Christmas is one of her handmade gifts. One year she painted the home of each neighbor on a clear Christmas ornament, for instance. I would love to tell you all our neighbors now follow Jesus, but that's not real. What I can tell you is we have seen gospel fruit and God has given us such great relationships with our neighbors as we seek to bring joy to them.

What about *work associates*? Do you think about your coworkers? I hope this book has helped you here.

Look at the next circle. Do you have *acquaintances*, people who aren't necessarily friends, but people you know? Another question I like to ask people is to think about their list of contacts on their phones. Think about yours. Can you identify at least three people in your contact list who don't know Jesus but with whom you have enough of a relationship that you could invite them to a meal or to have a cup of coffee and they would join you?

The final circle represents *person X*, or that person you don't know you may encounter. This could be someone sitting next to you in an airplane or at a coffee shop. It could be a server in a restaurant or someone at the bank. I'll be honest: 90 percent of the witness training I received in my young adult years focused on witnessing to strangers door-to-door or those we encounter whom we do not know. I'm grateful for that, but I hope you see the importance of sharing Jesus with the very people God puts in our lives. These dear souls are neither incidental nor accidental in your life.

If we're honest, one of the greatest hindrances to our sharing Jesus is simply this: most of us don't know enough people who don't know Jesus.

When we don't spend time with actual people who don't know Christ we can easily create stereotypes. The longer we hold to them, the less and less like reality they look.

Once we have gospel fluency and understand the story of Jesus, the best way to learn to share Jesus with people is to share Jesus with people. It's that basic.

Talk to a Real Person about Your Real Relationship with a Real Jesus

Think of the most terrifying situation for witnessing you can imagine. What would it look like? For some, it's cold-call, door-to-door evangelism.

Recently some of my students told me they'd never gone door-to-door, and asked if I would go with them. "Yes!" I said. I hadn't been able to do this for almost two years because back issues prohibited me from the walking and standing involved, so I was happy to join them. We went out on a Thursday late afternoon into a subdivision in North Raleigh.

The first person we met was a gang-banger with a knife as big as a baseball bat and a facial expression more menacing than a hungry pit bull. Next we stepped into a domestic dispute that required a quick call to 911. One of the students told me he thought he would surely lose his life that day.

Okay, I made all that up. We actually had a ball and met friendly people, because we were friendly ourselves. Most folks weren't home, and we didn't get to have many conversations in any depth. Still, we were able to speak to several, pray for a few, and leave materials with many.

The response of the students blessed me. Just going out and being in the community helped them a lot. They saw that people really are friendly; on this day no one was upset we came to see them. Some were very happy to see us. Students remarked at how easy this really is; what is hard is getting past the ideas we have based on our assumptions, our fears, and a lack of experience.

I reminded them door-to-door is just about the least effective method out there, and encouraged them to take what they learned to share with people they already knew. Cold-call evangelism is still better than what most people do, which is nothing. I don't personally do cold-call, door-to-door evangelism after dark. We don't live in Mayberry anymore.

Witnessing is like going to the gym; half the battle is getting there. Most people are more committed to fitness goals by learning more about health and fitness and by actually getting a plan to help them achieve their goals. In the same way, growing in your witness involves learning more: first, the gospel, and then ways you can talk about Christ out of who you are, and then the actual learning that happens by talking to others.

I want you to talk to real people where they are, not imaginary people holding a position you can't refute.

Principle 7: Talk to the actual person in front of you about the Jesus inside you; let them see and hear the change Jesus makes in you.

Interacting with People Where They Live

Imagine you are at a dinner party filled with people you don't know. You came with a friend, but you are a stranger to most of the people there. The host of the party speaks, sharing a story of her life. She walks all of you through a snippet of her personal history, telling you about her child who faced significant challenges early in life. You don't know her, yet there is something about the look on her face as she speaks, the truth of her story, and the way she connects with you when your eyes meet. You realize this person you didn't even know an hour before has made a significant connection with you.

This is the beauty of sharing Jesus. God takes a normal, broken person, just like you. He takes all of who you are, good, bad, and ugly, and through the inner work of the Holy Spirit and your growing love for Jesus, connects you with another person in a way that is truly remarkable. God uses people just like you to impact people just like those you know for his glory.

"Our age is quite simply the greatest opportunity for Christian witness since the time of Jesus and the apostles, and our response should be to seize the opportunity with bold and imaginative enterprise,"[44] Os Guinness argues in his book *Fool's Talk*. But he added the great need we face: "We have lost the art of Christian persuasion and we must recover it."[45] He observed how some have given up on evangelism and pursued social justice and other issues in its place.

You don't have to be a genius to speak about Jesus. You don't have to wow most people with your profuse Bible knowledge or your ability to talk about fundamental philosophical issues like the question of evil. You do have to care. You need to share the truth of Jesus with passion, and out of a life that cares for God and for others.

Sooner or later, we all think about where we came from, how things got started, or how we got here. These are all truth questions relating to one's intellect, but we usually think of them on a more emotional level, don't we? Instead of thinking philosophically about how the world got here, we want to know why we aren't taller or a better singer, or why we worry all the time. But those questions ultimately go back to design, or where things came from. We all experience the reality of brokenness all the time.

We all hope our kids won't grow up to be gangsters. We hope our car will crank in the morning. We hope to enjoy our jobs a long time, or to find a job we enjoy. People hope a lot and talk about hope a lot more. It's not so hard to move a conversation about hope to our hope in Christ.

Or you can simply talk about Jesus—how you love him, how he has changed you. Believe me, there aren't enough people doing that.

Answering Objections People Give

There will be times when you will clarify things to a person with doubts. Most of us worry about this a lot more than we actually encounter it because most of us aren't talking to many people about Jesus. The greatest need is Jesus, and the greatest thing we can offer someone is a relationship with him.

What if you are in a conversation and someone asks you a question about things like the problem of evil, many possible ways to God, or something like that? There is a myriad of fantastic books to help with this, but I want to give you a few things to help in those times. Guinness reminds us, "We should always give honest answers to honest questions, but we should know from the start that we can never give complete and convincing answers to every question."[46]

As we converse with people about the good news of Jesus, we want to do a couple of things in the process of telling them the good news: (1) remove roadblocks along their journey of life that keep them from seeing the story of Jesus; (2) raise questions in their minds about their current view of life.

It's beyond the scope of this book to give a proper treatment of apologetics and its role regarding evangelism; I do, however, encourage you to read books that will help you in that regard. I recommend two in particular: Os Guinness's *Fool's Talk*, which gives a fascinating look into the relationship between evangelism and apologetics in our time, and Timothy Keller's *The Reason for God*,[47] which offers answers to key questions from both a scholarly and a pastoral perspective.

Here are a few foundational truths to keep in mind as you have evangelistic conversations:

First, the very fact that you are having a conversation with someone instead of simply trying to give a presentation impacts the objections raised. Treating the person with whom you talk as an equal and truly listening to them will generally keep them from being defensive and raising unnecessary questions.

> The Bible's purpose is not to give you every answer you want. The Bible is God's revelation to us to show us his great plan and his great kingdom.

Second, the Bible never says we are to answer every question a person asks. The Bible's purpose is not to give you every answer you want. The Bible is God's revelation to us to show us his great plan and his great kingdom. It's not a reference book, though it speaks truthfully on a myriad of subjects; it's the great story that makes sense of all of life. That's not to say we shouldn't help answer ultimate questions of life that people raise. But witnessing is the sharing of a gospel story that changes everything.

Third, the gospel, not your answers or arguments, is the power of God for salvation. Don't forget that. They may not have every question answered, but they must hear the good news where they live.

Fourth, most questions people offer (about 80 to 90 percent in my experience) are not the actual reason they refuse to follow Christ, which is another reason to focus on communicating the gospel. We do want to answer honestly the real and sincere questions people have as we can, but we must get underneath the surface excuses people raise to deal with the genuine issues people have. We are not seeking to simply "close the deal" and get people to respond; we want them to meet Christ.

I recorded a video explaining briefly how to handle objections and questions. You can see it here: bhacademic.com /sharingjesus.

No matter how winsome and loving and clear you are, some won't receive Christ. And on rare occasions some may even become hostile. The latter is far less likely than you think, but Jesus is worth facing that, is he not?

It's vital for you to remember that no matter how effective at gospel conversations you become, or how attractive your witness, most will not respond positively to the gospel. Jesus told us the way to destruction is wide, and the way of salvation is narrow (Matt 7:13–14). There are plenty of times in the Gospels when people chose to walk away from Jesus rather than follow him.

The Power of a Changed Life: More than Words

I'm going to make a statement that may surprise you, given the fact that I'm a professor of evangelism. Sometimes, particularly with those in the inner circles you identified above, the best transition to the gospel is not to make one at all, at least verbally; it's to live in such a way as to create a hearing for it. Whenever we have the opportunity and sense the Spirit leading us to speak of Christ we should always do so. God is doing more than we know; we are merely a part of his bigger work. I say this with caution, because I know the force of the temptation to look for any reason possible not to speak about Jesus.

Sharing Jesus involves our verbal witness to be sure, but it includes more. Paul said in 1 Thessalonians 1:5 that the gospel came "not only in word" (ESV). It came with words, but not only with words. The more intimately we know someone, the more our lives matter and the less our words carry the impact. Look at 1 Peter 3:1–4, which gives the one time in the Bible where we are encouraged to impact others for Christ but at the same time told not to do so with words:

> In the same way, wives, submit yourselves to your own husbands so that, even if some disobey the word, they may be won over without a word by the way their wives live when they observe your pure, reverent lives. Don't let your beauty consist of outward things like elaborate hairstyles and wearing gold jewelry, but rather what is inside the heart—the imperishable quality of a gentle and quiet spirit, which is of great worth in God's sight.

Peter is not forbidding a wife to speak about Jesus, but when you are in such an intimate relationship as a husband and wife, you can't be preaching at your spouse all the time. In other words, how you live the gospel before close family matters much more than the words you speak.

On the other hand, if you have only a superficial relationship with someone, the words you speak with urgency matter
greatly. George Whitefield, the great evangelist of the First
Great Awakening, wrote: "God forbid that I spend a quarter of
an hour with anyone and not speak to them of Christ."[48] In the
book of Acts we see many examples of believers encountering
people and quickly and boldly proclaiming Jesus. In the text in
1 Peter 3, Peter is describing a long-term, intimate relationship
with a nonbeliever.

The greater the intimacy of a relationship, the more valuable your demonstration of a changed life, and the less intimacy, the more necessary is your verbal witness. As the picture
below illustrates, one's verbal witness should come early in
relationships. But, the more intimate the relationship becomes,
the more you serve someone and communicate the gospel
through your life and not just through words.

Maybe you are thinking this sounds all well and good,
but just what does this look like in our world? I had a student
named Alex who graduated from seminary, served in ministry,

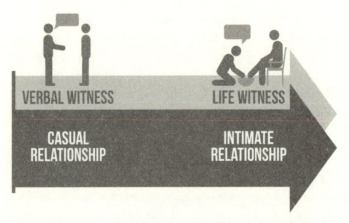

Note: verbal proclamation should always be a priority. This scale gives emphasis to the
increasing need for our life to reflect our words based on the intimacy of our relationships.

and then realized he was not called to vocational ministry. He went back into the world of finance, where he found his niche.

Alex worked very closely with his colleagues. As much as he wanted them to know Jesus, he knew if he brought up the gospel all the time they would stop talking to him. He developed the practice of five: as he interacted with coworkers, about every fifth conversation he had with one of them he would talk about Jesus. For his context that seemed to be about right: not too preachy, and yet not negligent of speaking of Christ. Let's face it, if you know someone really closely for years and never speak about Jesus, you *are* speaking about him: you are saying with your lack of words he is no big deal.

I shared Alex's practice of five with a group of businessmen who immediately saw it as a very helpful way to think about sharing Jesus in the workplace. I don't know what it is for you: five times, or three, or seven. I do know there is a balance between how you live the gospel and how often you speak it.

I read a compelling example of 1 Peter 3 in action in a sermon by Charles Spurgeon:

A husband who was a . . . depraved man of the world . . . had a wife who for many years bore with his ridicule and unkindness, praying for him day and night, though no change came over him except that he grew even bolder in sin. One night, being at a drunken feast with a number of his cursing companions, he boasted that his wife would do anything he wished—she was as submissive as a lamb! "Now," he said, "she has gone to bed hours ago. But if I take you all to my house at once she will get up and entertain you, and make no complaint." "Not she," they said, and the matter ended in a bet, and away they went! It was in the small hours of the night—but in a few minutes she was up, and remarked that she was glad that she had two chickens ready, and if they would wait a little she would soon have a supper spread for them. They waited, and before long, at that late hour, the table was spread, and she took her place at it as if it was quite an ordinary matter, acting the part of hostess with cheerfulness. One of the company, touched in his better feelings, exclaimed, "Madam, we ought to apologize to you for intruding upon you in this way, and at such an hour. I am at a loss to understand how it is you receive us so cheerfully, for being a religious person you cannot approve of our conduct." Her reply was, "I and my husband were both formerly unconverted, but, by the grace of God, I am now a believer in the Lord Jesus. I have daily prayed for my husband, and I have done all I can to bring him to a better mind. But as I see no change in him, I fear he will be lost forever—and I have made up my mind to make him as happy as I can while he is here." They went away, and her husband said, "Do you really think I shall be unhappy forever?" "I fear so," she said, "I would to God you would repent and seek forgiveness." That night patience accomplished her desire; he was soon found, with her, on the way to heaven![49]

You can see how the kind of Christianity displayed by this woman was more powerful than words, and opened her husband's heart to receive the gospel. If you think I'm suggesting a simple "out" for you to avoid speaking of Jesus, the reality is that truly loving people to Christ may be far costlier than just saying words.

This may explain why our words today seem not to have a lot of impact.

> Truly loving people to Christ may be far costlier than just saying words.

{ CHAPTER 8 }

Make Friends, Not Visits: Developing a Plan

We cared so much for you that we were pleased to share with you not only the gospel of God but also our own lives, because you had become dear to us.

—1 Thessalonians 2:8

My freshman year in high school in Alabama, I decided to get more serious about my physical fitness. At the time I was so skinny I had to run around in the shower to get wet. I could barely push one hundred pounds on the bench press machine at our makeshift school weight room. It was embarrassing, and I felt like a nobody, like a zero with the edges rubbed off. I got so sick and tired of being sick and tired, I devoted myself to becoming stronger.

I got a helpful push that year when my school hired a new head football coach. At the first meeting he had with all current and hopeful football players, he set a goal before us: every athlete on the team would eventually bench press three

107

hundred pounds. That sounded like an insurmountable goal, but for some reason it struck a chord with me.

As noted earlier with my book report fiasco in the ninth grade, I lacked self-confidence. I decided to go for this goal. That same year our school upgraded to a very nice weight room. Our coach gave us a plan for working out; off I went, following the plan religiously.

The next two summers a buddy and I rode our bikes the four to five miles to the school to lift. After football season we met the last period of the school day to pump iron as well. We got protein powder (no 'roids back then, thankfully) and worked hard. I got sidetracked a bit my sophomore year with a broken kneecap, but I picked up soon after.

It took time. Gains were often slow. But by my junior year, at a strapping 163 pounds, I did it. I lifted three hundred pounds!

One time. Ever.

I still have the "300-Pound Club" T-shirt from that accomplishment. I was one of the very first to make that goal. The guy who beat me won national championships playing football at Alabama. Did I play college football? Not a chance. I had two things going for me: I was too small, but I was also too slow.

I did make the weight-lifting goal, however, and it was a big deal. This marked the first time I could remember making a goal that required sacrifice and took years to accomplish. It gave me confidence in other areas of life as well.

> Sometimes the one thing that gets us from where we are to where we want to be is the conviction to stay focused on our goal of change.

Sometimes the one thing that gets us from where we are to where we want to be is the conviction to stay focused on our goal of change. It also helps to have a plan to help us get there.

It's true for most of us that when we are more disciplined physically we tend to be more disciplined in other areas of life, including our spiritual life. God wired us like that. We are not a collection of individualized compartments of life.

I hope this book has encouraged you to start a new path of sharing Jesus without freaking out. In this final chapter I want to challenge you to set a clear plan of life in terms of your witness. This is best done in terms of a larger life plan. I recommend Michael Hyatt and Daniel Harkavy's new book *Living Forward* or Tim Challies's book *Do More Better* to help with life as a whole.[50] I want to focus specifically on your lifestyle of witness, which you will live the rest of your life.

It's really not where you are that matters; it's where you are headed. This book aims to change your trajectory as a witness, and through this to grow you as a Christ-follower. It means you will think and live like a missionary every day of your life regardless of your location or vocation.

Vision, Plan, Execute

The vision for your life doesn't start with you; it starts with the God who created you. When you grasp the greatness of God's story, and that gospel story changes you, only then are you ready to live the life you were created to live. That's the big why of life: you and I were created to know and glorify God, and only through the work of Jesus for our salvation can we bring glory to him. Sharing Christ is a vital part of the journey. I see a lot of people today talking about becoming your best possible self. The way to do that is to be the person God created you to be.

The Christian life is not some nebulous journey with no forethought or planning. "Ready, fire, aim" may work in a pinch, but it's no way to live long term. When we see the big picture of the gospel we understand how God created each of us uniquely to glorify him based on who we are: gifts, talents, circumstances, all of that. Then we drill deeper to live daily lives hungry to bring glory to God and joy to others.

What does that look like for you? This is where we hear discussions about "finding the will of God" for your life. God's will is not lost! You "find" God's will by doing what you know to be God's will, and central to that are the Great Commandment and the Great Commission. The Great Commandment: loving God with all you are and loving your neighbor as yourself (see Matt 22:36–40) causes us to bring joy to those around us, and the Great Commission specifically helps us bring the greatest and most urgent news to those we meet.

In this final chapter I want you to develop a specific, practical, and personal plan for your daily life, focusing on sharing Jesus. God has given us the game plan already. The Great Commission in Matthew 28:19–20 tells us to make disciples, and the Great Commission is not the great suggestion! This includes winning people to Jesus, teaching them to obey all Jesus taught, becoming part of a local family called the church (which includes baptism, accountability, and community).

In Acts 1:8, Jesus' final words before his ascension, he gave a simple plan for all the church: receive the Spirit and be witnesses, and do so like this: to those near you (Jerusalem), to your region (Judea), to those you don't naturally like (Samaria—that is, don't leave anyone out), and to the ends of the earth. Our passion to reach people should extend to the nations.

Your plan needs to be rooted in the gospel and focused on Jesus, not on you, your church, or your method. Just as one plan for diet and exercise does not work for every person, you need to tailor your plan to the person God created you to be.

We all learn best what we put to practice the most. Our son Josh is a student pastor. Guess when he really began to ask me about communicating the Word to others? When he started preaching. Jesus saved you to be a disciple who makes disciples who makes disciples until Jesus returns.

We don't drift to godliness. We need a push and a plan. We don't drift to fitness; we need a push and a plan. Moses didn't drift to lead Israel (Exod 3–4); God gave him a push, and over time revealed a plan.

Remember when you fell in love, I mean head-over-heels, slap-your-face, hit-you-like-a-Mack-truck kind of love? When you met that person, you wanted to know him or her better, right? We do what we are passionate about and/or what we are pushed to do. We are best pushed to do what we are most passionate about.

A Plan to Change Your (Witnessing) Life

Witnessing means more than the passing on of information; it's helping people see the very meaning and essence of life and reality. This way we don't see people as projects we want to convert, but as God's image-bearers who desperately need to be made right with him, and that conversion is for God's glory and for their good. We don't see people as a project to conquer. Our desire to share Jesus with people is not because we want to convert them, but because *we* are converted!

> Our desire to share Jesus with people is not because we want to convert them, but because *we* are converted!

To change physically, we need a plan. The same is true spiritually. As a culture our dietary trajectory is not a good one, given the rise of processed foods and a parallel rise of issues such as diabetes and obesity. "We are literally killing ourselves," John Ratey says concerning physical health in his book *Spark*, adding, "What's even more disturbing, and virtually no one recognizes, is that [physical] inactivity is killing our brains too—physically shriveling them."[51]

Ratey offers the Naperville School District near Chicago as an example of a different approach. In this district, of the 19,000 sophomores, only 3 percent were overweight (compared to 30 percent nationally). But the students in this district are not only more fit. At a time when students in several Asian countries rank ahead of American students, the Naperville eighth graders ranked sixth in math and first in science in the Trends in International Mathematics and Science Study test, an international standards test taken by 230,000 students globally.

Why did this school district rank so well? Ratey observes one issue that stood out. What happened in Naperville didn't begin with a brilliant educator with a Mensa-level IQ. It started with a physical education teacher who read about the growing unhealthiness of American students. Naperville students shifted to begin their day with Zero Hour, a first period that included heart-rate monitors with students running a mile. What they discovered: learning is significantly enhanced when preceded by exercise.

These high school students were taught fitness principles and exercised their bodies before engaging their minds. In addition, each high school student developed his or her own personal plan for a life of wellness.

Here's my question for you: if a student at a public high school can develop a vision and plan for lifelong physical wellness, shouldn't you be able to develop a vision and plan for lifelong witness?

Principle 8: Developing a lifestyle of sharing Jesus consistently flows out of a plan to share Jesus regularly.

Principles for a Life Plan of Witness

Here are simple principles to set you on a journey of sharing Jesus:

First, focus your life on the gospel of Jesus Christ. All of life: spiritually, physically, emotionally, relationally, and financially. This is the *why* that undergirds all our lives. A daily, devotional, and practical focus on what Christ has done for you and desires to do for others keeps us focused. Sharing Jesus with others regularly starts with preaching the gospel to yourself daily.

Second, understand these factors that help your personal witness: giftedness, calling, and deep satisfaction. Over the years, people wiser than I have talked about the importance of bringing together one's giftedness, calling, and deep satisfaction to see practically how God made you and can use you for his glory.[52] Look at the Venn diagram featuring three interlocking circles representing these three. Developing a plan for your witness will involve you living at the center with all three at work.

Take a sheet of paper and write the three terms across the top in three columns. Underneath *Giftedness,* write what you understand to be your gifts. This includes spiritual gifts, but more. Include talents you have, personal characteristics, even limitations, as we talked about earlier. Your education, family, relationships, strengths all count in the area of giftedness. "Anything that enables you to do something effectively counts as a gift," Forster argues, which includes "much more than just your 'skills' and 'talents' narrowly understood. Personal characteristics, ranging from physical endurance to empathy, are gifts that empower you to do things others can't do."[53]

In the *Calling* category, write what you see as the greatest passions of your life. If you can think of specific things others have affirmed in you, like compassion, a love for the broken, a desire to teach the Word, or others, note those. What would you do for free? What is that thing you feel you must do with your life?

Concerning *Deep Satisfaction*, what are the things that bring you greatest joy? God built us for more than survival; he made us to long for something beyond us, something to bring deep satisfaction. Our ultimate satisfaction is in Christ! Out of that gospel-centered focus of life we can observe more specific and personal ways we find satisfaction. For me, as one called to teach, I take deep satisfaction in seeing people "get it," or discover something true that changes them.

Where these three meet, you find your sweet spot for serving Jesus out of the reality of who you are. For me, my giftedness would include some ability to communicate as a teacher, wonderful experiences that have helped me learn to share my faith, and great mentors. My calling includes a burden to equip leaders to live lives on mission for God. I get deep satisfaction when someone "gets it," or has a breakthrough in his life and witness (which is why I am a teacher, see?). What's yours? Think about ways you can utilize this information to communicate Jesus with others.

Third, from the Concentric Circles exercise earlier, identify in your circles of influence people you already know who don't know Christ. What would be the most practical ways of connecting with these people? How can you bring joy to their lives? Identify a realistic plan for connecting with at least one person in these circles weekly. This involves being open to random encounters with others and intentional meetings for conversations with others (those in the "person X" circle). It may be that one such encounter a week is realistic for you; volume matters less than consistency.

Fourth, regularly (monthly, quarterly) stop to assess your plan with an accountability partner or mentor. Perhaps find a fellow believer to join you in your witnessing efforts on occasion.

Finally, pray daily for your witness and for those to whom you will witness. This is spiritual work; nothing can substitute for prayer.

A final word: I mentioned at the beginning how I ask my students to rank themselves as a 1, 2, or 3 in terms of their witness. Another thing I ask them is this: Where do you believe God is leading you in ten years? It's my way of getting them to think of the trajectory of their lives. Look at today's date and add ten years to it. Don't think about suddenly talking about Jesus to everyone you see; just think about how you might talk about him more than you do now. What could your life look like in a month, a year, or a decade with that trajectory?

Epilogue

When is the best day to plant a tree?" I'd never thought about this until Fred, the owner of the orchard, asked me.

The answer? Twenty years ago!

"What's the second-best day?" he followed.

The answer? Today.

He told me that on the same day I bought fifteen pecan trees along with a few almond and apple trees from him. Michelle and I will enjoy those in our old age one day, but I wish I'd planted them years ago.

You may be thinking you've lost a lot of time as a Christ-follower when you could have been sharing Jesus with others but haven't. True, the best day to begin telling others the good news is the day you met Christ, but the second-best day to start is today. Don't put off any longer what you know to be true and good. Walk closely with God and dare to share your faith with great boldness!

The Principles

Principle 1: God created you for his glory, to advance his gospel with the gifts, talents, and opportunities he gave to you.

Principle 2: In order to share Jesus confidently and consistently with others, first share him confidently and consistently with yourself.

Principle 3: Shifting from giving an evangelistic presentation to having an evangelistic conversation takes pressure off the witness and relates the gospel more clearly to an unbeliever.

Principle 4: God has sovereignly placed you in this world at this time with the abilities and gifts you have to bring glory to him and show the joy of the gospel to others.

Principle 5: Effective evangelistic conversations connect the unchanging gospel with the specific issues people face.

Principle 6: Expect people to be open to the gospel, and learn to share Jesus where they live.

Principle 7: Talk to the actual person in front of you about the Jesus inside you; let them see and hear the change Jesus makes in you.

Principle 8: Developing a lifestyle of sharing Jesus consistently flows out of a plan to share Jesus regularly.

Endnotes

1. Name changed for privacy.

2. Jon D. Wilke, "Churchgoers Believe in Sharing Faith, Most Never Do," LifeWay, accessed September 2, 2016, http://lifeway.com/article /research-survey-sharing-christ-2012.

3. "Is Evangelism Going Out of Style?" Barna, December 17, 2013, https://barna.org/barna-update/faith-spirituality/648-is-evangelism-going -out-of-style.

4. Geoffrey Brewer, "Snakes Top List of Americans' Fears," Gallup, March 19, 2001, http://gallup.com/poll/1891/snakes-top-list-americans -fears.aspx. See also Peter Moore, "Argh! Snakes! America's Top Phobias Revealed," YouGov, March 27, 2014, https://today.yougov.com /news/2014/03/27/argh-snakes/.

5. Michael Green, *Evangelism in the Early Church* (Grand Rapids: Eerdmans, 1970), 175.

6. I got the idea of doing this from Tim Challies, *Do More Better: A Practical Guide to Productivity* (Minneapolis: Cruciform Press, 2015).

7. Gustaf Wingren, *Luther on Vocation*, trans. Carl C. Rasmussen (Philadelphia: Muhlenberg Press, 1957), 10.

8. This is developed similarly in Alvin L. Reid and Josh Reid, *Get Out: Student Ministry in the Real World* (Nashville: Rainer, 2015), 97–99; and Alvin L. Reid, *As You Go* (Colorado Springs: NavPress, 2013), 47–56.

9. These three relate specifically to popular movies in particular. For an encyclopedic look at seven fundamental plotlines, see Christopher Brooker, *The Seven Basic Plots: Why We Tell Stories* (London: Continuum, 2004). He identifies Overcoming the Monster, Rags to Riches, the Quest, Voyage and Return, Comedy, Tragedy, and Rebirth. He notes the best stories combine several of these; for instance, *The Lord of the Rings* combines six of the seven (all but comedy).

10. Eric Geiger, Matt Chandler, and Josh Patterson, *Creature of the Word: The Jesus-Centered Church* (Nashville: B&H, 2012), 84. My son Josh and I unpack this in some detail as well in our book *Get Out*, 97–98.

11. Geiger, Chandler, and Patterson, *Creature of the World*, 85.

12. "Life in 6 Words: The Gospel," YouTube video, 5:07, April 19, 2011, http://lifein6words.com.

13. "Two Ways to Live: The Choice We All Face," Matthias Media, accessed September 16, 2016, http://matthiasmedia.com.au/2wtl/2wtl online.html.

14. Living Waters Publications, The Way of the Master Television website, accessed September 19, 2016, http://wayofthemaster.com/; see the Free Tools menu.

15. Christianity Explored, Christianity Explored Ministries, accessed September 16, 2016, http://christianityexplored.org/Groups /274683/Home/Courses/Christianity_Explored/Christianity_Explored .aspx.

16. Tobin Perry, "Pastors Use 3 Circles Tool to Share Gospel, Train Members," North American Mission Board, August 2014, https://namb .net/news/pastors-use-3-circles-tool-to-share-gospel-train-members.

17. Robinson, Robert. "Come Thou Fount of Every Blessing," in *A Collection of Hymns used by the Church of Christ in Angel-Alley, Bishopsgate*, 1759.

18. Elahe Izadi, "The Powerful Words of Forgiveness Delivered to Dylann Roof by Victims' Relatives," *Washington Post*, June 19, 2015, https://washingtonpost.com/news/post-nation/wp/2015/06/19/hate -wont-win-the-powerful-words-delivered-to-dylann-roof-by-victims-relatives.

19. Name changed for privacy.

20. Tim Chester and Steve Timmis, *Everyday Church: Gospel Communities on Mission* (Wheaton: Crossway, 2013), 76.

21. This section is adapted from Alvin L. Reid, *Evangelism Handbook: Biblical, Spiritual, Intentional, Missional* (Nashville: B&H, 2009), 264.

22. This is a term used by my friend Jonathan Dodson, author of *The Unbelievable Gospel* (Grand Rapids: Zondervan, 2014).

23. See "Gospel Fluency," Soma, February 18, 2013, http://wearesoma .com/resources/watch/gospel-fluency/.

24. Tim Chester and Steve Timmis, *Total Church: A Radical Reshaping around Gospel and Community* (Wheaton: Crossway, 2008), 63.

25. This is also developed in Reid and Reid, *Get Out: Student Ministry in the Real World*, 96.

26. Chester and Timmis, *Everyday Church*, 113.

27. Selene Yeager, *Ride Your Way Lean* (New York: Rodale, 2010), 5.

28. Greg Forster, *Joy for the World: How Christianity Lost Its Cultural Influence and Can Begin Rebuilding It* (Wheaton: Crossway, 2014), 75–76.

29. Simon Sinek, *Start with Why* (London: Penguin, 2009).

30. Forster, *Joy for the World*, 94; emphasis added.

31. Name changed for privacy.

32. I'm grateful to Seth Godin for his thoughts on this subject from "Seth Godin on When You Should Start Marketing Your Product, Service,

or Idea," interview by Robert Bruce, Copyblogger FM, podcast audio, May 18, 2012, http://rainmaker.fm/audio/lede/seth-godin-marketing/. I've expanded and applied his essential thoughts on mass production and marketing to the church.

33. The following is adapted from Alvin L. Reid, *Evangelism Handbook: Biblical, Spiritual, Intentional, Missional* (Nashville: B&H Publishing Group, 2009), chaps. 10 and 11.

34. J. D. Greear, *Jesus, Continued . . . : Why the Holy Spirit Inside You Is Better than Jesus Beside You* (Grand Rapids: Zondervan, 2014).

35. Sherry Turkle, "The Flight from Conversation," *New York Times*, April 21, 2012, http://nytimes.com/2012/04/22/opinion/sunday /the-flight-from-conversation.html.

36. You can see how my friend Jonathan Dodson and I think similarly on this. He lists five similar ways to converse about the gospel in a way that is believable: 1. Ask questions; it isn't just about giving answers. 2. Focus on the heart, not just on the mind. 3. Steer conversation, with love and wisdom, toward deeply held beliefs and desires. 4. Value and affirm the insights of skeptics and seekers. 5. Tell stories from—and to—the heart. See Jonathan K. Dodson, *The Unbelievable Gospel: Say Something Worth Believing* (Grand Rapids: Zondervan, 2014), 47.

37. Name changed for privacy.

38. I unpack these concepts more in *As You Go*, 95–97.

39. Bruce Riley Ashford, *Every Square Inch: An Introduction to Cultural Engagement for Christians* (Bellingham, WA: Lexham Press, 2015), Kindle edition, Kindle locations 537–40.

40. Ibid., Kindle locations 684–88.

41. Jim Collins, *Good to Great: Why Some Companies Make the Leap . . . and Others Don't* (New York: HarperCollins, 2001), 17–40.

42. From a conversation with Jonathan, July 14, 2015. Go to bhacademic .com/sharingjesus to watch the conversation.

43. W. Oscar Thompson Jr., *Concentric Circles of Concern*, with Carolyn Thompson Ritzmann, rev. Claude V. King (Nashville: B&H, 1999).

44. Os Guinness, *Fool's Talk: Recovering the Art of Christian Persuasion* (Downers Grove, IL: InterVarsity Press, 2015), 17.

45. Ibid.

46. Ibid., 37–38.

47. Ibid.; Timothy Keller, *The Reason for God: Belief in an Age of Skepticism* (New York: Penguin, 2008).

48. Malcolm McDow and Alvin L. Reid, *Firefall 2.0: How God Has Shaped History through Revivals*, rev. ed. (Wake Forest, NC: Gospel Advance Books, 2014), 177.

49. C. H. Spurgeon, "A Word for the Persecuted" (sermon), August 16, 1874, Metropolitan Tabernacle, London. Transcript available at http:// spurgeongems.org/vols19-21/chs1188.pdf.

50. Michael Hyatt and Dave Harkavy, *Living Forward* (Grand Rapids: Baker, 2016); Tim Challies, *Do More Better* (Minneapolis: Cruciform, 2015).

51. John Ratey, *Spark: The Revolutionary New Science of Exercise and the Brain* (New York: Little, Brown, 2008), 4. See also Reid, *As You Go*, 198–99.

52. Again I'm indebted to Greg Forster for his discussion on this, although he too notes many godly leaders have observed this triune understanding of how God made us. See Forster, *Joy for the World*, 168–69.

53. Ibid., 169.

Eight Week Challenge

Introduction

The Eight Week Challenge is a way for individuals, small groups, and seminary classrooms to interact with the teaching and principles in *Sharing Jesus without Freaking Out*. The purpose is to answer the question: So now what? Now that I know to connect with people's pain or passion, what are the next steps? How do I walk out a life of evangelism in my context? In this Eight Week Challenge, we're going to make this teaching personal so that at the end of eight weeks you are well on your way to a lifestyle of evangelism.

These short, weekly segments were created for busy folks. In a few minutes each day—whether first thing in the morning, over lunch, or after the kids are in bed—you can walk through the practical steps that will help you learn how to share Christ and to do it on a regular basis. Just like with diet and exercise, a life of evangelism is a lifestyle change, not a quick fix. Be prayerful and diligent but also patient with yourself as you move through the next eight weeks. And remember: this is all for God's glory and your good.

Week 1

Principle 1: God created you for his glory, to advance his gospel with the gifts, talents, and opportunities he gave to you.

Scriptures to Meditate on:

"For God has not given us a spirit of fear, but one of power, love, and sound judgment." (2 Tim 1:7)

"Go, therefore, and make disciples of all nations, baptizing them in the name of the Father and of the Son and of the Holy Spirit, teaching them to observe everything I have commanded you." (Matt 28:19–20)

Questions for Reflection and Application:

1. What freaks you out in general?
2. What freaks you out or holds you back from sharing your faith?
3. What is the absolutely worst thing that could realistically happen if you spoke to someone about Jesus this week? (Hint: it's probably not going to!) Now, what's the most wonderful, amazing thing that could happen if you did?
4. If you were raised in a Christian home, was evangelism part of your family culture? How so?

5. Do you know the names of your neighbors? Do you know them well enough to know the pains or passions of their lives?

6. How different would your life look if you started living each day, just that day, passionately pursuing a life that glorifies God?

7. What is the one thing that keeps you from that? What is one thing you can do today to move toward that goal?

8. Reflect on this statement: "If you feel like you should share Jesus with someone, it's probably not the world, your flesh, or the devil. Take the risk."

9. Think about someone you know who doesn't know Jesus. Write their name down. Pray for him or her. (You don't even have to witness this week but it's okay if you do!)

10. Ask God to reveal to you what holds you back from sharing your faith. Then ask God for the grace to overcome that fear, believing he will do it.

This Week, Pray for:

- God to help you face and overcome your fears.
- God to help you meet your neighbors if you haven't already, and begin developing relationships with them.
- Each day this week, pray the three-fold prayer of the witness:
  a. God, give me this day: an opportunity to share Christ
  b. The wisdom to see it
  c. The courage to take it

Week 2

Principle 2: In order to share Jesus confidently and consistently with others, first share him confidently and consistently with yourself.

Scriptures to Meditate on:

"For I passed on to you as most important what I also received: that Christ died for our sins according to the Scriptures, that he was buried, that he was raised on the third day according to the Scriptures, . . ." (1 Cor 15:3–4)

"My soul, bless the LORD, and all that is within me, bless his holy name. My soul, bless the LORD, and do not forget all his benefits. He forgives all your iniquity; he heals all your diseases. He redeems your life from the Pit; he crowns you with faithful love and compassion. He satisfies you with good things; your youth is renewed like the eagle." (Ps 103:1–5)

Questions for Reflection and Application:

1. Have you ever thought about yourself as an evangelist for good news? Think back over something you've shared on social media or with good friends or family in person. Was it stressful or was it natural and fun?
2. Look again at the story of the gospel. What are the four major points of the gospel story plotline? Can you see how they relate to movie plotlines?

3. Think about a favorite movie. Why do you love it so
    much? How does it move you? How does your favorite
    movie reflect God's epic in Scripture?

4. Think through how you can naturally make a connection
    between your favorite movie and God's redemption of the
    world. Practice sharing that story with yourself this week in
    preparation for sharing it with others.

5. Do you have an authentic, growing relationship with
    God? Are you talking to him daily? Are you reading his
    Word regularly? Does a relationship with him excite you?

6. In Psalm 103, David is stirring himself up. He's remind-
    ing himself of God's faithfulness and kindness. How have
    you experienced God's benefits? Spend some time each
    day this week remembering specific ways you've experi-
    enced God as *great, glorious, good,* and *gracious.* Maybe it
    was that time you were laid off and each month—despite
    the fact that there was less money coming in than bills to
    be paid—you were somehow able to pay each bill in full.
    Maybe, after years of prayer, you finally met the person
    who would become your spouse or you were able to have
    children or you landed your dream job. Maybe it's finally
    seeing fruit bear in a severed relationship after decades
    of investing and waiting on God. Maybe it's remember-
    ing the ways God showers us with his love in the details
    of our lives—the rainbow after a funeral, the call from
    out of the blue from a friend when you needed it most,
    a surprise check in the mail that met a need you'd never
    mentioned.

This Week, Pray for:

*   God to continually grow your understanding of the won-
    der of the gospel.
*   God to grow your desire to share the gospel with others.
*   God to give you his love for those around you.

Week 3

Principle 3: Shifting from giving an evangelistic presentation to having an evangelistic conversation takes pressure off the witness and relates the gospel more clearly to an unbeliever.

Scripture to Meditate on:

"Paul stood in the middle of the Areopagus and said: "People of Athens! I see that you are extremely religious in every respect. For as I was passing through and observing the objects of your worship, I even found an altar on which was inscribed: "To an Unknown God." Therefore, what you worship in ignorance, this I proclaim to you. The God who made the world and everything in it—he is Lord of heaven and earth—does not live in shrines made by hands." (Acts 17:22–24)

Questions for Reflection and Application:

1. Where is a place you love to meet people for conversations? Starbucks, Cracker Barrel, an activity like hunting?
2. Have you ever introduced two people you love to one another? Maybe at a wedding or on a blind date or informally over coffee. Was it scary or did you enjoy it?
3. What are the three things people can tell about us in a conversation? Spend some time this week observing this in people you meet. Did the checkout guy at the grocery

store (or your waiter or a casual acquaintance) care
about you as a person?

4. As you observe if others genuinely care about you, also
   observe if your actions reveal if you care about others.

5. Over the next seven days, pay attention to how often and
   in what ways people talk about their pain or their passion. This includes anything from trivial matters to serious, life-altering events. Write down several examples.

6. Reflect on these instances and how the good news
   of Jesus can speak to these points of passion or pain.
   Practice connecting that person's situation to Jesus.

7. Even though we're three weeks into our study, I'm still
   not asking you to stand on a street corner wearing a card-
   board sign saying Jesus is coming! We're taking small and
   deliberate steps here toward a lifestyle of evangelism.
   Spend this week continuing to look for opportunities
   and ways to share Jesus in everyday conversation with
   others.

This Week, Pray for:

- God to help you see the opportunities to connect with
  others in everyday conversations.
- God to help you grow in your witness.
- Pray about developing a long-term relationship with
  at least one unbeliever at your work, school, or in your
  neighborhood.

Week 4

Principle 4: God has sovereignly placed you in this world at this time with the abilities and gifts you have to bring glory to him and show the joy of the gospel to others.

Scripture to Meditate On:

"But you are a chosen race, a royal priesthood, a holy nation, a people for his possession, so that you may proclaim the praises of the one who called you out of darkness into his marvelous light. (1 Pet 2:9)

Questions for Reflection and Application:

1. God did not make a mistake when he uniquely created you and positioned you in this world. List at least three specific ways you can see God has wired you for his glory and the good of others. Are you a good listener? Do you love meeting new people? Do you enjoy talking about sports, music, or the arts? We tend to look only at our weaknesses. Take a few minutes to thank God for the good gifts he has given you.

2. Name at least one limitation in your life you would change if you could.

3. How can God use that limitation for his glory? Perhaps you came from a troubled home as a child and, although you still have struggles at times, you can joyfully share

how Jesus has helped you through your past. Or maybe you have battled cancer or some other crisis and the struggle in one area has actually made you stronger in another.

4. Think about and articulate *why* you want to share your faith. Is your *why* big enough?

5. What are the things in your life that stir your affections for Jesus? What are the things that diminish your affections for him? What is one thing you can pursue or remove that will bring you closer to God?

6. How is sharing the gospel different from selling a product?

7. How can you bring the joy of God to others around you? Keep in mind your abilities, gifts, and current circumstances. Who is someone already in your life that you can bring joy to this week? How will you do so? Maybe it's paying for the fast food meal of the person behind you in line. You might volunteer to help a neighbor with yard work. Or you could simply provide a listening ear to a coworker struggling with a family issue.

This Week, Pray for:

*   God to help you grow in your ability to share Jesus.
*   Pray by name for your neighbors, friends, and family who don't know Jesus. If you still don't know anyone, ask God to introduce you to those already in your life who don't know him.
*   Ask God to open your eyes and ears to how you can creatively bring joy to others.
*   A way each day to encourage at least one person.

Week 5

Principle 5: Effective evangelistic conversations connect the unchanging gospel with the specific issues people face.

Scripture to Meditate on:

"Love one another. Just as I have loved you, you are also to love one another. By this everyone will know that you are my disciples, if you love one another." (John 13:34)

Questions for Reflection and Application:

1. Let's take a quick inventory of where our prayer life is today.
   - Are you praying regularly for God to help you live the gospel well?
   - Are you asking God each week to help you grow in your witness?
   - Are you praying daily and specifically for any unbelievers or asking God to introduce you to an unbeliever?
   - Are you still battling fear and/or insecurity in sharing the gospel? If so, are you willing to ask God each week to increase your desire to share Jesus with others?
   - Are you proactively partnering with God in prayer or is there someway you can be more diligent in this area?

2. Which of the five approaches seems most natural or appealing to you? Why?

3. Can you think of a person you know where that approach might help?

4. This week, seek to utilize one or more of these approaches in an evangelistic conversation. Reflect on the experience afterwards. What went well? What was hard?

5. Consider keeping a journal or record of what you're praying for and your progress in sharing your faith.

6. Pay attention to when the thought of Jesus comes to mind in a conversation. Be bold and starting talking about Jesus as you think about him.

This Week, Pray for:

- God to help you live the gospel well.
- God to fill you with his love for people.
- God to help you use one of these approaches in an evangelistic conversation with someone.
- God to help you love and affirm a non-believer you know whose lifestyle you wouldn't necessarily endorse.

Week 6

Principle 6: Expect people to be open to the gospel, and learn to share Jesus where they live.

Scripture to Meditate on:

"A woman of Samaria came to draw water. 'Give me a drink,' Jesus said to her. . . . 'How is it that you, a Jew, ask for a drink from me, a Samaritan woman?' she asked him. For Jews do not associate with Samaritans. Jesus answered, 'If you knew the gift of God, and who is saying to you, 'Give me a drink,' you would ask him, and he would give you living water.'" (John 4:7–10)

Questions for Reflection and Application:

1. Ask a friend, coworker, or family member to tell you his or her story. Or, if you know the person well, to catch you up on his or her story. How might you empathize with that individual's story, seeing ways your story relates to his or hers? How might you retell that person's story from the perspective of being changed by Jesus?
2. Think of a sphere of life you care a lot about (music, work, sports, and so on). Listen carefully when others talk and consider how you can relate it to the gospel story. For example, you could ask a coworker why they

work at your company. If they say it's fulfilling, talk to them about how our desire to live a fulfilling life comes from our Creator, and share the gospel story. If they complain about how they hate their job, show them how our pain comes from a broken world, and share how the gospel brings hope in the midst of a frustrating world.

3. Do you expect others to be open to hearing about Christ? If you don't, spend time reflecting on the root of that belief.

4. How do you see evangelism? Are you making new friends or are you making new contacts? Is it about relationships or about numbers? Is sharing Jesus about listening and loving others well, or is it about performance?

5. Are you actively expecting God to do great things in your neighborhood, workplace, home, and school?

6. How can you empathize with the brokenness others are experiencing? Where are the pain points in your own life and how has Christ has rewritten your story? Think through how to share an example of God's transforming love and power from your life with an unbeliever.

7. Reflect on a past conversation with an unbeliever. Did you show that other person empathy, love, and compassion? Or did you judge him/her for language, dress, level of ignorance, or lifestyle?

8. Reflect on your recent encounters with unbelievers. Did you start with them, engaging them where they are? If not, how could you have done so? Remember, this isn't about being down on yourself, this is about growing in our witness. Thoughtful reflection is a key ingredient to becoming better at sharing our faith.

This Week, Pray for:

- An expectation that people are open and eager for the gospel, and that God is going to do something great in your context.
- God to help you understand where someone is at and engage with him or her right in that moment.
- God to give you growing discernment to pick up on when people speak about their pain or their passion.

Week 7

Principle 7: Talk to the actual person in front of you about the Jesus inside you; let them see and hear the change Jesus makes in you.

Scripture to Meditate on:

"In the same way, wives, submit yourselves to your own husbands so that, even if some disobey the word, they may be won over without a word by the way their wives live when they observe your pure, reverent lives. Don't let your beauty consist of outward things like elaborate hairstyles and wearing gold jewelry, but rather what is inside the heart—the imperishable quality of a gentle and quiet spirit, which is of great worth in God's sight." (1 Pet 3:1–4)

Questions for Reflection and Application:

1. When you think of evangelism, what automatically comes to mind? Is it sharing the gospel with the random person you sit next to on the plane? Is it knocking on the front doors of complete strangers? Do those closest to you come to mind?
2. Reflect on whether or not you believe you have to know the answers to all the questions before sharing the gospel. Think through how you will respond to someone when you're asked a question you don't know how to answer.

3. What does it mean to show Jesus by the way you live?
    Think about the ways you've experienced others living
    out their faith without words.

4. Reflect on this statement: *The closer you are to someone, the
    less your words matter and the more your actions matter.* What
    is one way you can better love those closest to you today?
    Think of times like family reunions when you are around
    unbelieving family members. Instead of obsessing over
    how you will drop the gospel on them, what are ways you
    can serve them?

5. Think about your experience talking to others about
    how Jesus has changed your life. Can you identify a
    rhythm or pattern that works well for you? Maybe, like my
    friend in finance, you're intentional about sharing a faith
    experience every fifth time you've talked to someone. If
    you don't see a pattern yet, ask God to help you identify
    what works best for you in your context.

6. Look again at the list of people you recorded from the
    Concentric Circles exercise. For whom are you most bro-
    ken over their salvation? What might you do this week to
    show and to share Christ with that person?

7. Think about someone you know very well who doesn't
    know Jesus. How might you show them Jesus in your life
    even as you share him with your lips?

This Week, Pray for:

-   God to help you identify a witnessing rhythm that's right
    for your context.
-   God to show you how to demonstrate the gospel by your
    life even as you share good news with your lips.
-   God to help you see how costly it is to live a life that con-
    sistently shows the radical change the gospel makes, and
    to help you live like that.

Week 8

Principle 8: Developing a lifestyle of sharing Jesus consistently flows out of a plan to share Jesus regularly.

Scripture to Meditate on:

"'Follow me,' he told them, 'and I will make you fish for people.'" (Matt 4:19)

Questions for Reflection and Application:

1. Is your life focused on the gospel? How do you plan to preach Jesus to yourself daily and speak of him to others regularly?

2. Do you understand your giftedness, calling, and those things that bring deep satisfaction? What are the abilities and gifts God has given you? (Family? Friends? What are you good at?) What are the things you must do? (Help broken families? Create art? Help people learn?) What deeply satisfies you at the end of the day?

3. What are ways you can share Christ out of the sweet spot of these three categories? For example, do you share the gospel by listening or talking? I have a friend who is naturally gifted at offering wise counsel to others. He feels called to care for those struggling emotionally. He gets great satisfaction in seeing people overcome emotional hurdles. It's no surprise he's helped numerous people

come to Christ in the context of helping them deal with their past.

4. Identify people in your Concentric Circles. What is a specific way to share with at least one person from this list weekly?

5. Are you meeting regularly with an accountability partner or mentor? Spend that time focusing on moments you do well sharing your faith, not on moments where you may have missed an opportunity.

6. Reflect on where you are in your commitment to sharing the gospel. Can you commit to the plan we outlined in this chapter? Why or why not? What concerns or worries do you have?

7. What specific ideas, truths, people, or principles has God placed on your heart over the past eight weeks?

8. As you think about all you've learned over these weeks, write down your evangelism goals. Where do you want to be in six months? One year? Ten years?

9. How can you make evangelism part of your family culture?

10. Write out in one paragraph a summary of your plan for regularly sharing Christ in conversations with others.

This Week, Pray for:

- God to prepare you, to use you, and to work in the lives of those you meet.
- God to cement these lessons in your heart and help you discern wise goals as you continue on your witnessing journey.
- God to continue to grow you in your witness and open your eyes and heart to the people he puts in your path who need him—for his glory and your good.

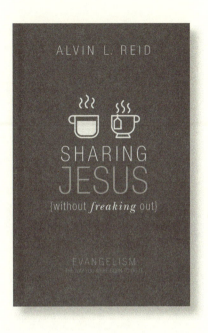

For videos and other resources related to

Sharing Jesus without Freaking Out,

please visit
bhacademic.com/sharingjesus